SELF-PUBLISH YOUR BOOK

using

FREE

SOFTWARE

SELF-PUBLISH YOUR BOOK

using

FREE

SOFTWARE

SELF-PUBLISH YOUR BOOK
using
FREE SOFTWARE

ISBN: 978-1-957418-19-3

Published by:
ELDERSLIE PRESS
172 Peck Hill Road
Woodbridge, Connecticut 06525
United States of America

CONTENTS

INTRODUCTION

A DECISION FACED BY ALL FLEDGLING AUTHORS is how to get their book published. There are thousands of people who want to be authors, and together I'm sure they write millions, if not billions, of words every year. ALL of these hopeful authors are competing against each other as well as against books published by established authors and mainstream, commercial publishing juggernauts. There aren't any major, traditional publishers who accept unsolicited manuscripts from rookie writers. The only way to get a manuscript accepted by a major publisher is through an agent — but most agents are overwhelmed with manuscripts and queries, too, so the odds are heavily against even getting an agent to read your manuscript if you are a new author who doesn't have a solid track record.

The invention of print-on-demand delivery for printed books has revolutionized the publishing industry and made it possible for thousands of amateur and undiscovered writers to not only see their books in print, but to see them offered for sale on the Internet through vendors such as Amazon, Barnes and Noble, and a host of others. Amazon KDP is the biggest player in this field, by a significant margin, but there are reasons why authors might choose either to use another service to publish their book, or to release their book through multiple vendors simultaneously. This book isn't about how to decide which print-on-demand service to use. That's a marketing decision, and each author's situation and expectations are different, making it a very personal decision, as well.

Once an author makes the decision to self-publish, the next decision to be made is how to create the manuscript and, after that, how to take the finished manuscript from a raw computer file to a final format that's ready to be uploaded to Amazon KDP or another print-on-demand service. It can be done in Microsoft Word and, in fact, I have written a book that explains exactly how to do it using Word. But Microsoft Office is an expensive program (or suite of programs), and not everyone can afford it. Beyond that, while a word processor such as Word is good for writing the raw manuscript, there are a great many experts (both real experts and self-professed experts) who proclaim that in order to properly format a book for print you have to use expensive software such as Adobe *InDesign* or a program called *Scrivener.* Other experts advise authors who want to self-publish to use a free program from Amazon called *Kindle Create.* There are other programs, too, that can be used to transform a raw manuscript into a finished book layout; some are free, while others are commercial software that are available only by purchase or subscription.

I'm the first to admit that a program such as *InDesign* is invaluable if the end product is going to be an expensive, high-end book for which the minute, intricate details of the book's interior formatting are as important as the book's content. For most self-published authors, that's simply not the case. *InDesign* is expensive — very expensive. And it's not for sale; *InDesign* is only available by subscription, which means to use it you have to rent it, at a cost of $239.88 per year (or more, depending on the plan). That's a lot of money for most beginning authors, and the monetary cost doesn't consider the extra time needed to learn how to use the software.

We just want to tell the story, and get it out there so that people can read it. Ideally, we want it to look professional enough that a reader's first impression when they open the book won't be, "Oh, my God! This book must have been created by a kindergartner!" Fortunately, we don't need *InDesign*; we can accomplish that using the same word processing software we use to write the manuscript. It's not even difficult; it just requires taking a few minutes, and caring enough about the work to make it look as professional as possible. Not only that, the good news for people who can't afford or who don't want to spend the money to buy (or subscribe to) Microsoft Office is that there are entirely *free* programs available that can not only facilitate drafting the manuscript, they can also be used to format the book to be print-ready. The result, all from one *free* program, will be good enough that only a professional book designer will know your book wasn't designed by a professional.

There are two *free* programs that rival Microsoft Word in features and flexibility: LibreOffice, and SoftMaker FreeOffice. Both are office suites that include a word processor, a spreadsheet, and a presentations program. LibreOffice also includes a drawing program and a database but, since the major tool for producing a book is the word processor, that's what this book will focus on. Although LibreOffice is more widely known than FreeOffice, my comparisons have demonstrated that FreeOffice is a smaller program that runs more efficiently on older computers. The word processor module in FreeOffice is called TextMaker. This book will explain how anyone can use FreeOffice TextMaker to write, format, and self-publish their book, from manuscript to final upload, without having to spend *any* money to buy software.

Let's get started.

SELF-PUBLISH YOUR BOOK

using

FREE

SOFTWARE

1 — GETTING THE SOFTWARE

THE COMPANY BEHIND FREEOFFICE is named SoftMaker Software GmbH. They are headquartered in Nuremberg, Germany. SoftMaker publishes and sells software that includes professional fonts, a PDF editing and viewing program, and the SoftMaker Office software suite, which is available for outright purchase or on a subscription basis for Microsoft Windows, MacOS, Linux, Android, and iOS. FreeOffice is a completely free version of the SoftMaker Office suite that the company distributes entirely free as an introduction to the SoftMaker Office suite. FreeOffice offers most — but not all — of the features found in the paid version of the software. The good news is that, once you download the software and install it, you can use it for as long as you want.

There is a web site for FreeOffice, which is completely separate from the main SoftMaker web site, which is found at: https://www.freeoffice.com/en/. FreeOffice allows installation on up to three devices on one license, and that can be a mix of Windows and Mac devices. Upon download, it is required that users register the software with the company and obtain an activation code — which is free.

What are you giving up in comparison to the full, paid version? Surprisingly, not a lot, at least in terms of features that matter for self-publishing.

FreeOffice is only available (for Windows) in a 32-bit version. The difference between 32-bit and 64-bit programs is how much computer memory they can utilize. Unless you are working with a huge book, this won't matter at all.

FreeOffice doesn't allow users to customize the menus, but it does offer a choice between a classic menu similar to Word 2003, and a ribbon-style menu similar to Word 2007 and newer. Personally, I prefer the classic menu system but most users today will probably choose the ribbon-style menu — which is the default.

FreeOffice includes automatic hyphenation and spell-check, but no grammar checker or thesaurus. It reads and writes both .doc and .docx file formats (used by Microsoft Word), as well as the .odt file format (used by LibreOffice) and SoftMaker's own, proprietary file format. I have my copy set to use the .docx format as the default file format. FreeOffice has the built-in capability of exporting to PDF (but not to PDF/A). The paid version also allows exporting directly to the .epub digital book format; that's not possible in FreeOffice, but there are ways to accomplish that for free. It also includes a sidebar, which will be discussed later. FreeOffice also allows tracking changes.

That's a lot of functionality in an entirely free software package.

Obtaining the software is as simple as downloading the installation file and running it. Follow the prompts to obtain an activation code, then enter the activation code the first time you start the software … and that's all there is to it. There is a user manual that's available on-line through the program. I have found that it's more convenient (for the way I work) to download the user manual as a PDF so I can have it available on my computer even if I'm not on-line.

Once the software has been installed, there should be three new icons on the Windows desktop: one for TextMaker (the word processor app), one for PlanMaker (the spreadsheet app), and one for Presentations (the equivalent to Powerpoint).

2 — THE MANUSCRIPT

ONCE THE SOFTWARE HAS BEEN INSTALLED, it's time to write the book. TextMaker offers some tools to make that job easier. When the sidebar is activated, it displays the paragraph styles and character styles, which facilitates formatting. (In the paid version, the sidebar can also be used for document navigation, which is more useful during the actual writing stage. This is one of the features sacrificed in making FreeOffice free.)

As in Microsoft Word, TextMaker has a built-in spelling checker that underlines in red any words that aren't found in its dictionary. My experience using the grammar checker built into Microsoft Word was that the grammar checker was totally useless, and I disabled it because it interfered with my style of writing. For this reason, I don't view the lack of a built-in grammar checker in TextMaker to be a negative at all. Writers who feel they might want the assistance of a computer grammar checker can use an app called *Language Tool*.[1] A free version of *Language Tool* is available that runs on-line, in your web browser, and there is also a free desktop app that can be downloaded for use under Windows or macOS.

I happen to be a visually-oriented person so, unlike most writers, I prefer to set up the format for a book before I start. This allows me to actually see how the book is going to appear to

---

[1] https://languagetool.org/

readers as I progress. This approach is more suitable for non-fiction, especially for books that will include illustration, photos, and/or charts and graphs. For writing a novel, it is probably less constricting to start working on a standard 8½ by 11 page size using Times New Roman as the font in 11-point or 12-point size, and simply write. All that can be changed during the formatting stage, so there is no need to be concerned about it while writing the story.

If you plan to submit the manuscript to agents or commercial publishers, then it should be set up in a standard manuscript format. If the publisher or agent has their own format requirements, be sure to follow them. If there are no specific requirements, the following criteria are a good starting point:

- Set the margins to 1-inch all around — top. Bottom, and both sides
- Use Times New Roman 12-point type
- Indent the first line of each paragraph ½ inch
- Set the line spacing to double space
- Use left justification only. Do not use full justification
- Put a header at the top right, including your last name, a dash, the title, a dash, and the page number
- Use ONE space after a period, not two. (Using two spaces after periods is a carry-over from the days of mechanical typewriters.)
- Begin each chapter on a new page, with the chapter number and/or title about one-third of the way down the page

- Show breaks in the action or timeline within a chapter with a blank line, with the # symbol centered on the line
- To finish the manuscript, put "The End" on a separate line following the last line of the text.

The first page of the manuscript will be the title page. This page does not get a header or a page number. The title page should include:

- The author's name and contact information in the upper left-hand corner. Include telephone number and e-mail address.
- The book title and sub-title, between one-third and one-half down the page, center-justified
- The author's name again (or pen name, if used, also center justified)
- The word count

That's the basic layout for a manuscript. Most agents and publishers will either accept this format, or have their own requirements which should be very similar to these.

~ ~ ~ ~ ~

As in Microsoft Word, when TextMaker is set to use inches as the unit of measurement the default paragraph style is called "Normal" and the default tab stop spacing is one-half inch. Do NOT use the tab key to indent the first lines of paragraphs. Instead, modify the "Normal" paragraph style to automatically indent the first line. To accomplish this, be sure the sidebar is visible, with the paragraph styles displayed. Select the "Normal" style, and click the "Edit" box near the bottom of the sidebar panel:

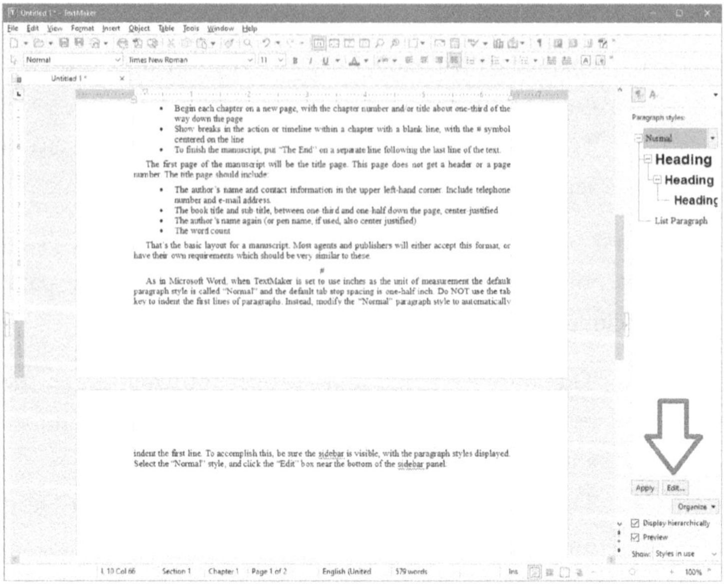

This opens the pop-up dialogue box in which you can set the parameters for the "Normal" style.

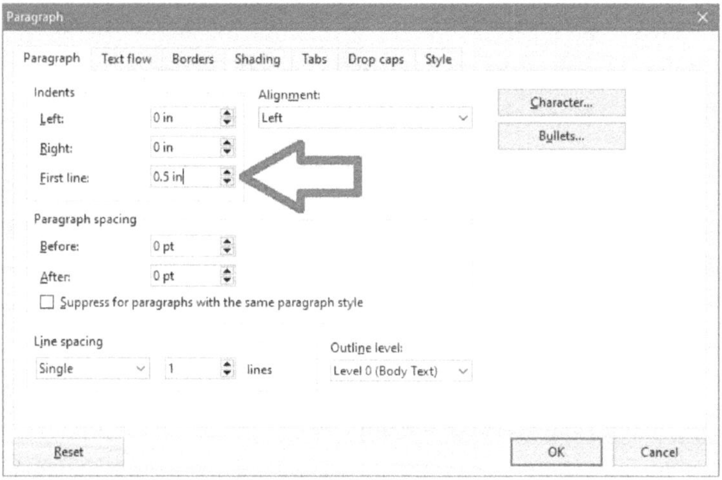

When it's time to format the book interior for print, the styles will become more important. For just writing the manuscript, this is all that's needed.

Each new chapter should begin on a new page. There are multiple ways to accomplish this; one is just plain wrong, one is okay (maybe), and the third is the one I recommend:

1. DON'T just keep hitting the enter key (line breaks) to keep entering blank lines until the text jumps to the new page. That way is wrong by anyone's criteria, but there are people who still think of a computer word processor like a fancy electric typewriter who do this. Just … DON'T.
2. The second way to jump to a new page is to hold down the CTRL key and press the ENTER key. This inserts a page break code into the file. This feature works exactly the same in TextMaker as it does in Microsoft Word, so people familiar with Word will have no trouble doing this one. This method is ideal for manuscripts and for simple novels, in which the headers and footers will be the same on every page for the full length of the manuscript or book. Where this method fails is when formatting a book for print when each chapter needs to have a different heading (perhaps indicating the chapter title). Changing headers for each chapter requires using a section break rather than a page break.
3. The third way to jump to a new page is to insert a section break. This will become important during formatting for print, but I'll mention it here to finish out this discussion. This works slightly differently in FreeOffice than it does in Word. To insert a section

break with a page jump in TextMaker, we use the Insert>Break>Chapter Break command. This is found on the "Insert" tab of the ribbon menu, at the extreme left-hand end. Click the small down arrow beneath the word "Break," then click the last choice: "Chapter."

~ ~ ~ ~ ~

Now it's time to start writing. Once the manuscript has been completed and edited, it will be time to take the finished manuscript and format it for print if you aren't going to submit it to agents for publication through the traditional publishing route.

3 — TRIM SIZE

THE FIRST STEP IN FORMATTING ANY BOOK for print is deciding what size the book will be. In book publishing, this is referred to as "trim size." The name derives from the way printed books are produced and assembled. The individual pages are printed on larger sheets of paper that each typically hold four printed pages. These larger sheets are called *folios*. The pages are slightly larger than the intended final size of the book. They are folded and then bound together to create the book. After assembly, the edges are trimmed to the final size.

Choosing a trim size is both an art and a science. All of the popular print-on-demand services offer a range of standard trim sizes from which to choose. Amazon KDP allows custom trim sizes but, since other print-on-demand services do not, unless you plan to offer your book exclusively through Amazon it is best to use one of the standard trim sizes that all the services offer.

The basic rule of thumb for determining what trim size to use is to look at other books of the same type or genre as your book fits into, and to choose a trim size that the majority of your competition uses. There's a reason for this. This is not a situation where it's good to stand out from the crowd. There are a lot of books available today. People who read books of a particular genre become accustomed to a general size and style, so a new book that's drastically different from what they have read and enjoyed in the past is less likely to appeal to these potential buyers. If you don't know what size other books of the same genre are, spend a few minutes at a bookstore or in the books aisle at the local supermarket with a ruler or a tape measure to find out what size publishers are using for books in the same genre as your book. (This is also a good opportunity to get a feel for the types of cover design popular for that genre, but that is beyond the scope of this book.)

The following are some general criteria for trim size:

5" x 8"	Novellas (short novels); general fiction
5.25" x 8"	General fiction
5.5" x 8.5"	Fiction and non-fiction
6" x 9"	Fiction and Non-fiction; longer books

(Larger pages help reduce page count). Some sources say 6" x 9" is the most commonly used trim size for books in the United States.)

Not even all those sizes are offered by all three of the most popular print-on-demand services: Amazon KDP, Barnes and Noble Press, and Draft2Digital. Amazon KDP and Barnes and Noble Press both offer all four trim sizes in paperback, but they only offer 5.5" x 8.5" and 6" x 9" in hardcover. Draft2Digital does not offer the 5.25" x 8" trim size. For maximum flexibility in printing and distribution, this means it is best to choose a trim size of 5" x 8", 5.5" x 8.5", or 6" x 9".

If your proposed book is something that you think will fall into the "mass market" category (those smaller books that are often found in revolving racks at convenience stores and similar outlets), Barnes and Noble Press offers the following standard trim sizes:

4" x 6"
4.25" x 7"
4.37" x 7"

Neither Amazon KDP nor Draft2Digital offers any of those sizes as standard trim sizes. Amazon KDP allows custom trim sizes, which will allow matching one of those sizes if you wish to publish through both Amazon KDP and Barnes and Noble Press. Draft2Digital does not appear to offer custom trim sizes.

To further confuse the issue, although Barnes and Noble Press says the 4.25" x 7" size is the "mass market" trim size … it isn't. I have measured many mass market paperback books, and the most customary trim size by an overwhelming margin is actually 4.13" x 6.75".

There is also a new trim size that several mass market publishers have recently introduced to the marketplace: what Kensington Publishing Corporation has named the "Mass Max" format. This is slightly larger than the traditional mass market trim size, and the goal is to give prospective buyers a feeling that they are getting a bit more than what the traditional mass market size books offer. This new trim size is 4.75" x 7". At this time, none of the major print-on-demand services offer this as a standard trim size, and none of them appears to have any plans to introduce it. This means if you want to publish your book in that trim size, at the moment the only option is to use a custom trim size from Amazon KDP.

~ ~ ~ ~ ~

In TextMaker, the page size is set from the "Layout" tab on the ribbon menu, or from the "Page Setup" option under the "File" tab in the classic menu. In the ribbon menu, with the "Layout" tab selected, at the left side is the "Page setup" panel. Within this panel are the options for setting the page size, the page orientation, and the margins. Clicking on "Page size" opens a pop-up menu that suggests several standard paper sizes. None of these are suitable for book trim sizes but, at the bottom, there is an option for "More . . . ." Clicking on that opens another option box that allows you to specify the exact page size, to two decimal places of an inch.

Once you have chosen the trim size and set the page dimensions to that size paper, you are ready to set up the basic page layout.

4 — PAGE LAYOUT

ONCE YOU HAVE ESTABLISHED and formatted the trim size, the next step is to establish the margins and layout of the interior pages. Although each of the major print-on-demand services has slightly different criteria for these dimensions, it is possible to select a single set of dimensions that will work for all of them. But, first, we need to look at the terminology that applies.

Every page has a top margin, a bottom margin, and two side margins. For a single page, the side margins are simple "left" and "right." But a book is formatted with the pages viewed as pairs, so the names of the margins change. With the book held open, the side margins at the extreme left and the extreme right are referred to as the "outside" margins, while the two margins nearest to the spine of the book are referred to as the "inside" margins. The top and bottom margins, of course, remain the same.

Word processing programs default to a single page layout; the format has to be changed for a book layout with facing (or "mirrored") pages. In SoftMaker FreeOffice,, choose the Layout Tab. From the Layout tab, click the small arrow in the lower right corner of the Page Setup panel. This opens a pop-up menu for Page Format. On the right-hand side, beneath where the margins are set, is a check box for Mirror Margins. Checking that box will change the margin settings from Left and Right to Inside and Outside.

The layout of a basic page includes the block of text that makes up the story (the book body), together with top, bottom inside and outside margins:

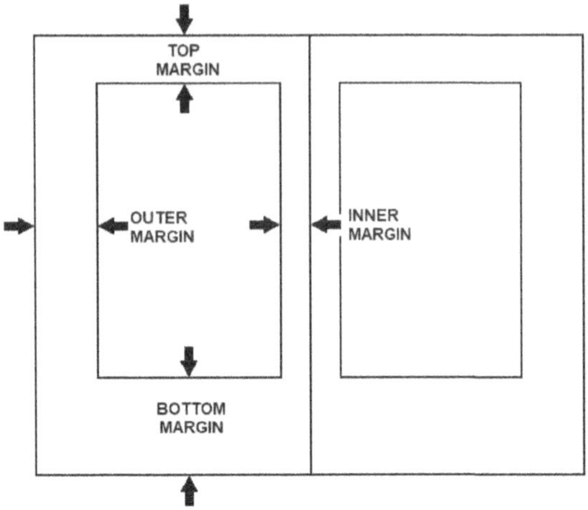

In a classically-designed book, the page layout considers both facing pages together and sets the inside and outside margins such that the two inside margins together equal the width of the outside margin:

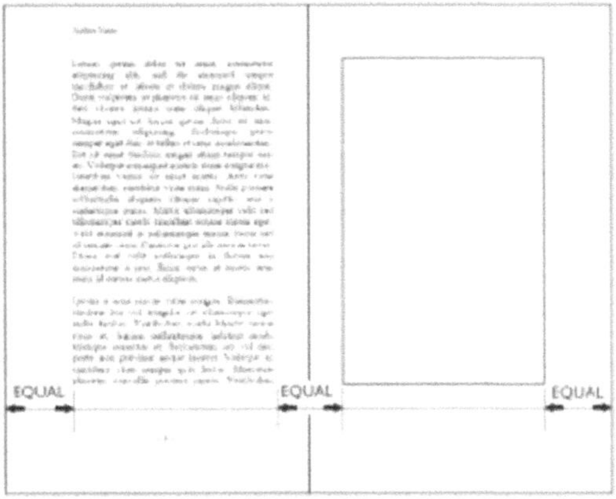

As a general rule, this means that the inside margins would be approximately half the width of the outside margins. But most books—especially paperback books—don't open completely and lie flat when opened. A portion of each page is glued or sewn together in the binding process, so when the book is opened the inside edges of the pages stay together and the reader can't view all the way to the absolute edge of the page. Book makers and book designers allow for the portion of each page that is "lost" to the binding process. This extra space is referred to as the "gutter."

The next diagram shows the same page size as in the previous two diagrams, but with the added gutter allowance shown to illustrate the concept:

For a self-published author, adhering to classical book design theories generally isn't the primary concern. Margins created according to classical layout guides are overlay large; this results in less text on each page, which means more pages and higher printing costs. For the typical book, the goal is to keep the margins as small as practical, while ensuring that the margins are wide enough to pass the printer's quality checks and also so the text doesn't appear to be uncomfortably crowded onto the pages. My experience has been that Amazon's guidelines for margins are slightly smaller than desirable (and, for longer books, I have found that margins set to Amazon's minimum dimension won't pass Amazons' own automated quality check). At the end of this chapter, I provide a table with what I have found to be workable margins for the three most common trim sizes. Using these dimensions should allow your book to look like a professional book, and to pass the quality checks on Amazon KDP, Barnes and Noble Press, and Draft2Digital. How to set the gutter dimension varies depending on what program you use.

You can also get an idea of what margins to use by looking at books for sale in the genre your book will fall into. Check a half dozen or so books and make note of what their margins are. If your margins are set to the same dimensions, your printed book will feel comfortable to readers of that genre.

To set the margins in FreeOffice, TextMaker, select the "Layout" tab, then click the small arrow in the lower right corner of the "Page Setup" panel. This opens a pop-up menu where you can enter the margin dimensions. In TextMaker, the gutter width is set independently from the margin dimensions.

Most books in print may have headers and/or footers on the pages, and this is another margin that different programs handle differently. In TextMaker, the top and bottom margins are set the same as in Microsoft Word, and they behave the same. The top and margin settings on the "Margins" tab of the "Page Setup" dialogue box are for specifying the distance from the top or bottom edge of the paper to the top or bottom of the main body of text on the page. The distance from the edge of the page to the header or footer is set on the "Layout" tab of the "Page Setup" dialogue box.

The dimensions set forth in the following table should work for all print-on-demand services. These dimensions are based on having headers that may include the book title, author, and/or chapter title in the header, with page numbers in the footer. For novels, some publishers save space by incorporating page numbers into the headers. In this case, the bottom margin can be reduced to perhaps 0.50" or even slightly less.

Suggested Page Layout Dimensions:

5" x 8"	Inner Margin	0.50"
	Outer Margin	0.50"
	Gutter	0.20"
	Top Margin	0.75"
	Bottom Margin	0.75"
	Header Margin	0.30
	Footer Margin	0.30
5.5" x 8.5"	Inner Margin	0.55"
	Outer Margin	0.55"
	Gutter	0.20
	Top Margin	0.75"
	Bottom Margin	0.75"
	Header Margin	0.30"
	Footer Margin	0.30"
6" x 9"	Inner Margin	0.60"
	Outer Margin	0.60"
	Gutter	0.20"
	Top Margin	0.75"
	Bottom Margin	0.75"
	Header Margin	0.30"
	Footer Margin	0.30"

5 — BOOK BODY FORMAT

Paragraph Format

The body text in a printed book should be set as fully justified, which means that the spacing of the words on each line is adjusted so the right edge on the block of text forms a vertical line just like the left edge. In proper terminology, text is "right justified," "left justified," "fully justified (both edges align), or "center justified." Most word processors just call it "justified" when referring to fully-justified.

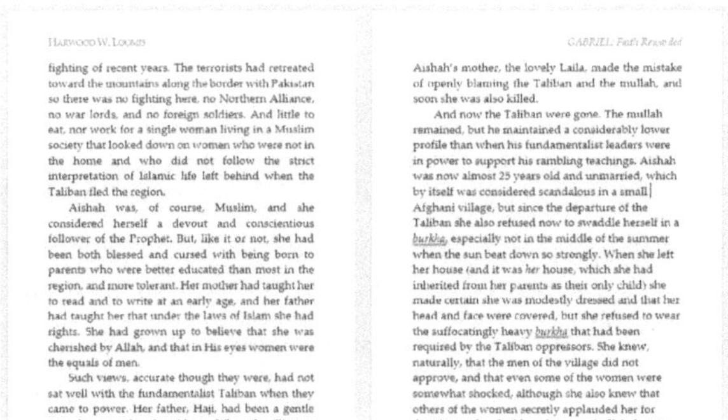

HARWOOD W. LOOMIS

fighting of recent years. The terrorists had retreated toward the mountains along the border with Pakistan so there was no fighting here, no Northern Alliance, no war lords, and no foreign soldiers. And little to eat, nor work for a single woman living in a Muslim society that looked down on women who were not in the home and who did not follow the strict interpretation of Islamic life left behind when the Taliban fled the region.

Aishah was, of course, Muslim, and she considered herself a devout and conscientious follower of the Prophet. But, like it or not, she had been both blessed and cursed with being born to parents who were better educated than most in the region, and more tolerant. Her mother had taught her to read and to write at an early age, and her father had taught her that under the laws of Islam she had rights. She had grown up to believe that she was cherished by Allah, and that in His eyes women were the equals of men.

Such views, accurate though they were, had not sat well with the fundamentalist Taliban when they came to power. Her father, Haji, had been a gentle man, but proud and stubborn. When the illiterate mullah put in place by the Taliban government told her father he must follow the Taliban's interpretation of the Qur'an "or else," Haji had defied him. Worse, he had ridiculed the "mullah" in public. Not long after, Haji was killed by unknown assailants.

2

GABRIEL: Faith Rewarded

Aishah's mother, the lovely Laila, made the mistake of openly blaming the Taliban and the mullah, and soon she was also killed.

And now the Taliban were gone. The mullah remained, but he maintained a considerably lower profile than when his fundamentalist leaders were in power to support his rambling teachings. Aishah was now almost 25 years old and unmarried, which by itself was considered scandalous in a small Afghani village, but since the departure of the Taliban she also refused now to swaddle herself in a *burkha*, especially not in the middle of the summer when the sun beat down so strongly. When she left her house (and it was *her* house, which she had inherited from her parents as their only child) she made certain she was modestly dressed and that her head and face were covered, but she refused to wear the suffocatingly heavy *burkha* that had been required by the Taliban oppressors. She knew, naturally, that the men of the village did not approve, and that even some of the women were somewhat shocked, although she also knew that others of the women secretly applauded her for dressing as they had heard women in Kabul were doing.

Aishah absently tied the rope to the handle of her bucket and dropped it down into the well, listening to hear when it reached the water. No problem there — the wait was no longer than normal.

3

In the sample above, the left page is fully justified, the right page is "ragged right"

The visual impact of justified text compared to "ragged right" is immediately obvious, and it says a lot about the quality of the book. It's an immediate clue as to whether a book was published by an amateur or by a professional who cares about his or her creation.

Harwood W. Loomis

fighting of recent years. The terrorists had retreated toward the mountains along the border with Pakistan so there was no fighting here, no Northern Alliance, no war lords, and no foreign soldiers. And little to eat, nor work for a single woman living in a Muslim society that looked down on women who were not in the home and who did not follow the strict interpretation of Islamic life left behind when the Taliban fled the region.

Aishah was, of course, Muslim, and she considered herself a devout and conscientious follower of the Prophet. But, like it or not, she had been both blessed and cursed with being born to parents who were better educated than most in the region, and more tolerant. Her mother had taught her to read and to write at an early age, and her father had taught her that under the laws of Islam she had rights. She had grown up to believe that she was cherished by Allah, and that in His eyes women were the equals of men.

Such views, accurate though they were, had not sat well with the fundamentalist Taliban when they came to power. Her father, Haji, had been a gentle man, but proud and stubborn. When the illiterate mullah put in place by the Taliban government told her father he must follow the Taliban's interpretation of the Qur'an "or else," Haji had defied him. Worse, he had ridiculed the "mullah" in public. Not long after, Haji was killed by unknown assailants.

2

Gabriel: Faith Rewarded

Aishah's mother, the lovely Laila, made the mistake of openly blaming the Taliban and the mullah, and soon she was also killed.

And now the Taliban were gone. The mullah remained, but he maintained a considerably lower profile than when his fundamentalist leaders were in power to support his rambling teachings. Aishah was now almost 25 years old and unmarried, which by itself was considered scandalous in a small Afghani village, but since the departure of the Taliban she also refused now to swaddle herself in a *burkha*, especially not in the middle of the summer when the sun beat down so strongly. When she left her house (and it was *her* house, which she had inherited from her parents as their only child) she made certain she was modestly dressed and that her head and face were covered, but she refused to wear the suffocatingly heavy *burkha* that had been required by the Taliban oppressors. She knew, naturally, that the men of the village did not approve, and that even some of the women were somewhat shocked, although she also knew that others of the women secretly applauded her for dressing as they had heard women in Kabul were doing.

Aishah absently tied the rope to the handle of her bucket and dropped it down into the well, listening to hear when it reached the water. No problem there—the wait was no longer than normal.

3

Fully-justified text looks neat. Left justified text looks "ragged," hence the name.

The paragraph format dialogue box is also where the information is entered regarding whether or not the first line of each paragraph in indented. Standard practice is to indent all paragraphs except the first paragraph following a chapter heading or major sub-heading. In professional book design the amount by which the first line is indented is an "em," which is a dimension equal to the width of a capital 'M' in the font being used. Word processing programs don't measure paragraph dimensions in ems, they use inches and decimals of an inch (or millimeters, in countries using the metric system). A good number to start with for the first line indentation is .20".

Another setting in the paragraph format dialogue box is line spacing. Like most word processors, TextMaker defaults to single line spacing. Depending on what font is selected for the printed version, single spacing may be acceptable. However, professional book designers usually prefer to add a bit of extra space between lines to open up the text so the pages don't look too dense. In print terminology this is usually expressed in terms such as "11-point type on 13-point leading." TextMaker allows two ways to do set this, both from the paragraph format dialogue box.

At the bottom of the box there is a place to set "Line spacing." The choices offered are "Single," "Multiple," "Exactly," and "At least." "Single" is self-explanatory. "Multiple" allows setting the line spacing to a multiple of the single line spacing, in decimals of an inch. Using this method of controlling line spacing, a setting somewhere between 1.10 and 1.20 may look better than single spaced. The other two choices, "Exactly" and "At least," change the measurement to points, as used by professional book designers. Using these, if the selected type size is 11-point Garamond, the spacing can be set to 13 points.

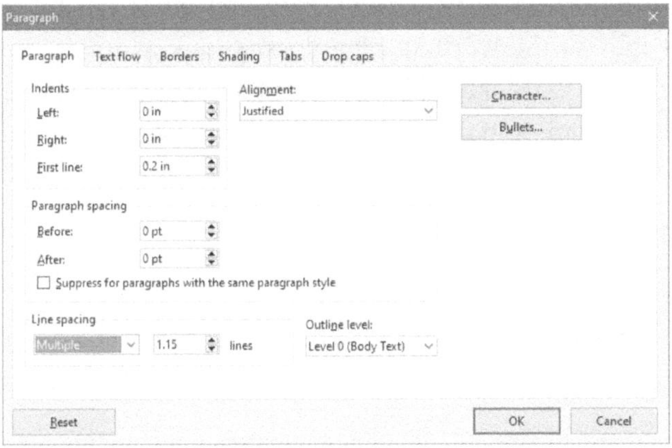

The paragraph format dialogue box is also where the vertical space before and after each paragraph can be set. In certain types of publications, paragraph breaks are indicated by extra spacing between paragraphs rather than by indenting the first line. For novels and for most general non-fiction books, no extra space should be added between paragraphs; the start of a new paragraph is indicated by indenting the first line.

If the type of book you are working on calls for using space between paragraphs, different programs measure it differently. Microsoft Word and FreeOffice TextMaker both measure paragraph spacing in points. You will have to experiment to see what looks best. For the best results with print-on-demand printing, do not use extra line breaks to create space between paragraphs. Use the paragraph format dialogue box to set the space there. The results will be better.

When text is fully justified, the word processing program adds space between words to force the right-hand end of each line to align with the right margin. If a sentence includes a number of long words, this can cause the spacing between words on some lines to be uncomfortably large. To resolve this, you can turn on hyphenation, which will allow long, multi-syllabic words to be split so the word spacing doesn't look as unpleasant. In FreeOffice TextMaker, this setting is found on the "Layout" tab, in the "Paragraph" panel. I always turn on hyphenation.

Headers and Footers

Most print books have headers or footers, and usually they have both. What the headers and footers contain is the book designer's choice. If you are self-publishing your own book—you are the book designer. What should go on the tops and bottoms of your pages?

Once again, the best advice is to go to a bookstore (or the books aisle in a Walmart or your local supermarket) and look at actual books in the same genre as your book. What do they put for headers and footers?

There is no requirement for anything other than a page number, and the page number can be located either in the header or in the footer. If the page number is placed in the footer, it is usually placed in the center of the page. Less often, the page number may be located at the outside margin. Don't place your page number on the inside margin—it's too hard to see it there when your reader is trying to find the place where he or she left off.

To give you a head start on your research, I checked a number of books in two genres to see if there was any consistent trend. What I found was that romance novels all seem to handle headers and footers pretty much the same. Looking at history books as examples of non-fiction, I found much less consistency.

In the category of romance novels, I looked at ten titles. Of those, three had the page number centered at the bottom of the page, five had the page number at the outside margin on the top of the page, and two combined the page number and the book's title or author at the outside margin on the top of the page. For the headers, seven had the author's name centered on the even (left-hand) pages and the title centered on the odd (right-hand) pages. One had the title centered at the top of the even pages and the author's name centered at the top of the odd pages. Two combined the page number and author's name at the outside margin of the even pages, and combined the page number and the title at the outside margin of the odd pages.

To make it easy, for general fiction books we can generalize that you won't go wrong to omit a footer (allowing you to reduce the bottom margin), place the page number at the outside margin in the header, place the author's name (you) centered in the header of the even-numbered (left) pages, and place the book title centered in the header of the odd-numbered (right-hand) pages.

For non-fiction, I looked at several books that fall generally into the category of "history." I avoided books that were aimed at children, books that were advertised as being for advanced placement history classes, and several that looked like memoirs or family histories rather than general audience history books. What I found was that, as with the romance novels, only one put the page number in the footer. All the others put the page number in the header, at the outside margin. Beyond that, there was little consistency. About half put the author's name centered in the header of the left-hand pages and the book title centered in the header of the right-hand pages. The others put the book title centered in the header of the left-hand pages, and the chapter title centered in the header of the right-hand pages.

I favor putting the book title in the header of the even-numbered pages and chapter titles in the header of the odd-numbered pages. Personally, I also favor putting the page numbers in the footer, but incorporating the page number into the headers allows eliminating the footers, reducing the height of the bottom margin and resulting in a few more lines of print per page, which reduces the total page count.

HOWEVER ... the *first* page of each chapter should *not* have a header. How can this be accomplished in TextMaker?

Fortunately, it's quite easy. TextMaker offers two ways to do this: manually, and automatically. The manual solution is found in the "Page Setup" dialogue box, under the "Chapter" tab. At the top of this box is a pair of check boxes under the "Master Pages" heading: "Different first page," and "Different left and right pages." Checking the first of these boxes allows omitting headers and footers from the first page of each chapter, while allowing headers and footers on all following pages. Checking the second box allows alternating headers on the left and right pages of each chapter.

Just below that, in the section under "Chapter starts on," you can set whether new chapters simply begin on the next page after the preceding chapter ends, or if you want the next chapter to always begin on a right-hand (or, less common, left-hand) page. In the United States, mass market books usually have chapters beginning on either page but high-end books more often always start new chapters on a right-hand page. If you check this option box, TextMaker will automatically insert a blank left page if the preceding chapter ends on a right-hand page.

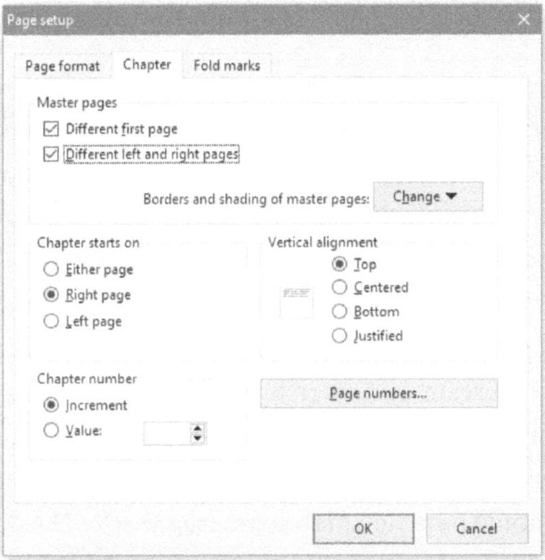

The Page Setup dialogue box, Chapter tab

In TextMaker, each chapter can have different headers and footers — or none at all. If headers and footers have been created for the first chapter, they will automatically be carried over as new chapters are created ... unless you want to change them. In non-fiction books, for example, instead of the author's name being the header on left pages and the book title being the header on right pages, often the title will be the header on the left page and the *chapter* title will go in the header on the right pages.

In order for all this to work properly, it is important — even critical — to create chapter changes correctly. In TextMaker, as with most word processors, pressing CTRL+ENTER creates a page break, with the following text beginning on the top of the next page. That is *not* what is needed to create chapter breaks. TextMaker provides several other kinds of breaks, which are accessed from the "Insert" tab on the ribbon menu. Under "Insert," the left-most panel is "Break." Clicking the small arrow beneath this open the "Breaks" options list. The last item is "Chapter." That's the one to use when ending one chapter and beginning a new chapter.

The new chapter will be opened, bringing in the same headers and footers that appeared in the previous chapter. If a new chapter needs a different header on either page, simply edit the header. Go back to verify that the headers haven't changed in the preceding chapters; they should remain undisturbed.

To further simplify the task of formatting a manuscript for printing as a book, paragraph styles can be formatted to *automatically* create a chapter break preceding any style. For a number of reasons relating to the way the print-on-demand services process files when they are uploaded, the title of new chapters should be assigned the paragraph style "Heading 1." The dialogue box for setting up this paragraph style allows setting the typeface, the font size, the justification, how much space to add above the title (this should be a large number, enough to move the title down about one-third of the page height), and the space after the title.

In the "Paragraph styles" dialogue window, select the "Text flow" tab. On that tab is a pair of options under "Pagination" that are not self-explanatory. Ignore the check box for "Column break" unless you are formatting a page with multiple columns. The other check box is the one we want: "Page break." What this setting does is to instruct TextMaker to *automatically* insert a chapter break immediately before whenever a line of text is set to the Heading 1 style.

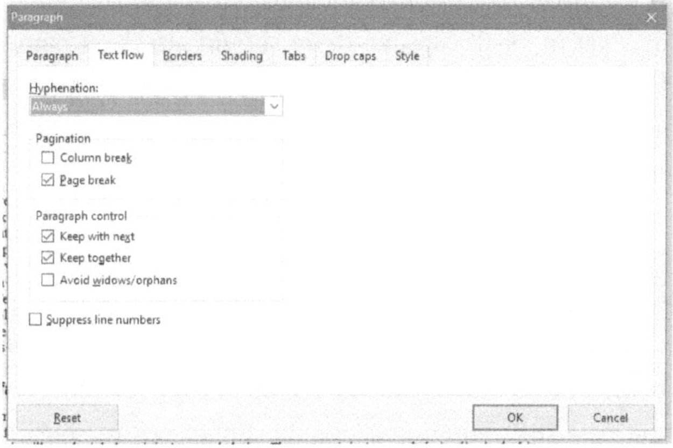

The Paragraph Style dialogue box, Text flow tab

It couldn't be easier. The next section will discuss the use of paragraph styles in more detail.

Using Styles

The major print-on-demand services all seem to agree that they prefer the manuscripts to use the styles function in your word processor rather than using "brute force" (such as using tabs or multiple spaces to create indented paragraphs, or multiple line breaks to move chapter headings down on the page). This is more important if you upload the book as a Word .docx file than if you upload a .PDF file, but using styles makes it much easier to modify the book design as you go, so it's a good idea to learn how they work.

For most books, the body will contain only a few different styles. For a novel, there might be one style for the chapter number, maybe one style for the chapter title (if you use chapter titles—many novels don't), and one style for the typical paragraphs. The opening paragraph of each new chapter is usually not indented, and may include a drop cap letter and/or a few lines set in small caps, so there should also be a paragraph style for the opening paragraph (this style could be named "First" or "First Paragraph," or something that you will recognize as the first paragraph of a chapter).

What can you set in the Paragraph Style dialogue boxes? Just about every aspect of the paragraph format. And, once you set up a style, highlighting any paragraph and then clicking on that style name automatically adjusts the highlighted paragraph to that style's attributes. When you have a style selected and you are entering new text, when you use the Enter key to start a new paragraph, the new paragraph will be in the same style unless you manually select a different style.

In the section on Body Text (above) I discussed the "Paragraph Style" menu. What's important to understand is that when you use the "Paragraph Style" menu, the settings affect only the current paragraph. When you go into "Format Styles" and change the format of a paragraph *style* (for example, the default

"Normal" style, the change automatically affects all paragraphs using that style, *and all paragraph styles that are based on that style.*

What does this mean? Assume the default "Normal" style uses the Times New Roman font in a 12-point style. Suppose you want to change the font for your printed book from 12-point Times New Roman to 11-point Garamond. One way to do this is to use the mouse to highlight the entire book and then make the change. But that's a problem if you have headings and subheads that use a different font and type size, because you *don't* want to change those. The solution is to use Format Styles to edit the Normal paragraph style to use the Garamond font in an 11-point size. Make the change once, and all paragraphs using the "Normal" style should automatically update. If you have a "First paragraph" style set up and it is based on the "Normal" style, all the first paragraphs in each chapter should also update. If you later decide to try using a Baskerville font instead of Garamond — again, make the change once using Format Styles and the change should be made automatically throughout the entire book.

CAUTION: As you work with documents that have been copied from other documents and then edited, the number of styles has a tendency to proliferate. This makes your work more cumbersome. It's always best to keep your default document template free of all styles other than the default styles. Begin new documents from the default template, create only the styles you will need for that document, and save that document. If you will be writing multiple books in the same genre, you can create a new template or master document for books, with defined styles you'll need for your books, and save that template separate from the word processor's default template.

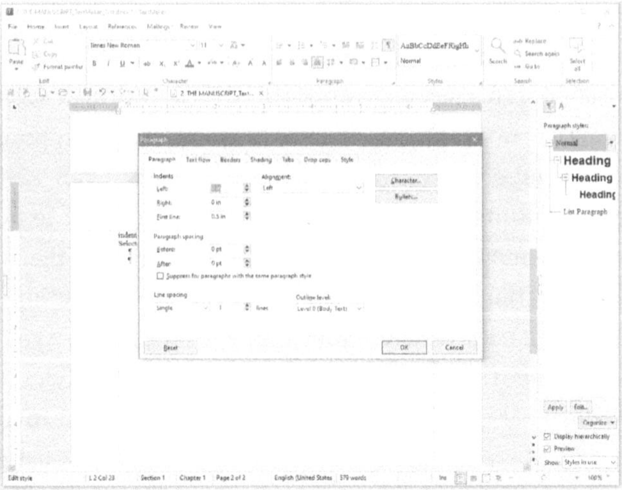

The Modify Style dialogue box

With the styles displayed in the sidebar, highlighting a style and then clicking "Edit" below the list opens the "Paragraph Format" dialogue box — but now any changes will affect not only the current paragraph, but ALL paragraphs that use that style.

Widows and Orphans

In book design, "orphans" are when the first line of a new paragraph or a section subhead falls by itself on the bottom of a page, and "widows" are when the last line of a paragraph appears by itself on the top of a new page. Widows and orphans detract somewhat from reading speed and comprehension, and should be avoided. Major word processing programs all have a setting to eliminate widows and orphans automatically.

In SoftMaker TextMaker, widow and orphan control will be found in Format > Paragraph > Text Flow.

Widow and orphan protection only works for multi-line paragraphs. It can't prevent a one-line subhead from being stranded at the bottom of a page, but this is also something that should be avoided. Remember: no matter how powerful your word processing software is, always be sure to go through the entire manuscript and check every page for errors after the document has been formatted for the final layout and trim size.

Common Errors and Bad Habits

Every key stroke in your manuscript adds to the size of the file, so it's important to not put in anything that you don't need. Beyond that, using the keyboard to enter spaces, characters, and other formatting by the "brute force" method instead of using styles may result in your book not looking the way you expected it to when you upload the file to the print-on-demand service. Some common errors to avoid include the following:

- Don't use spaces or tabs to indent the first line of your normal paragraphs. Use the style format to set the indentation of the first line.
- Only enter a single space after each period that ends a sentence. Entering two spaces after periods is a carry-over from mechanical typewriters. With proportional typefaces, it isn't necessary and it's considered incorrect.
- Don't hit the Enter key twice to add space between paragraphs. Use the Style menu or the Format Paragraph dialogue to set the amount of space you want before and/or after paragraphs.
- Don't use spaces or tabs to try to center titles or subtitles on the page. Use the paragraph and style justification settings to control this.

6 — TYPOGRAPHY (FONTS)

ONCE THE PAGE LAYOUT HAS BEEN SET UP to your satisfaction, it's time to decide on what fonts you want to use for the main body text of the book, and for chapter headings. There are a lot of fonts available to any computer user, and the font you choose can make a big difference in whether your book is easy to read or hard on the eyes.

Fundamentals

It's best to use only two — or possibly three, at most — fonts throughout a book. Using too many fonts can overwhelm the reader's eyes and senses. In designing the interior of a book, the goal of the designer is to not draw the reader's attention to the design, or to the fonts. The goal is to make the book as easy to read as possible. Some fonts are simply more readable than others, so choosing the right font is an important decision.

Book design professionals and graphic artists have determined that for reading large blocks of text (such as a book), "serif" typefaces are better that "sans serif" typefaces. Let's begin by understanding what those terms mean.

A serif is a small transverse extension at the ends of the strokes forming each letter or character. "Sans" is the French word for "without," so a sans serif letter is a letter that does not have an embellishment at the ends of the strokes. For example,

in the fonts that seem to have become the effective default choices for many computers and for many computer users, Times New Roman is a serif typeface, and Arial is a sans-serif typeface.

First, it helps to understand the terminology. The style of the letters—the design—is properly called the "typeface." In the early days of printing presses, each individual letters was carved or cast on a separate block of wood or metal. The job of the typesetter was, quite literally, to set all those individual chunks of wood or metal in rows to make up words and sentences. The term "font" referred to a specific combination of typeface, type size, and attributes (such as italics or bold face). This means that, for example, Times New Roman is a typeface; Times New Roman 12-point Regular, Times New Roman 14-point Regular, and Times New Roman 10-point Italic are three separate fonts, even though they are variations of the same basic typeface.

Today, thanks to digital type technology, the term "font" has become largely interchangeable with "typeface." In the old days, a printer had to buy a box of type just for Times New Roman 12-

point Regular. If he also wanted Times New Roman 14-point Regular he had to buy another box of type. If he wanted Times New Roman 10-point Italic, he had to buy a third box of type. Today, computer users have a wide variety of typefaces available as standard with their operating system and, thanks to the magic of technology such as TrueType and OpenType, a single font can be scaled from too small to read all the way to too large to fit on a standard sheet or paper. We are blessed—and spoiled. We have so many fonts available to us, in fact, that deciding which to use can be an almost paralyzing decision.

Typeface Selection

For many computers and word processing programs, it seems that Times New Roman has become the default font (or typeface). Aspiring self-publishers can just use Times New Roman but, in reality, although it will get the job done it isn't a good choice. The reason it isn't a good choice lies in the history of the typeface.

The name itself reflects the history. "Roman" is often used to refer to the standard, vertical variant of a typeface. In 1931, The Times newspaper of London adopted a new typeface that was designed specifically for their use. It was for The Times, it was new, and the basic variation was the Roman font, so it became known as 'Times New Roman." Being intended for a newspaper, it was designed expressly to be legible in small type sizes and in the comparatively narrow columns found on the pages of newspaper. Consequently, although Times New Roman can be used to set an entire book, the letters are a bit narrower and the resulting text is a bit too compact for optimal reading when used to set an entire page.

I know two authors who have self-published novels set in Times New Roman, so it certainly can be done. That said, book design professionals generally recommend using other readily-available fonts to set the body text of books. Then the problem becomes deciding which font to use instead of good old Times New Roman.

The goal in font (typeface) selection is not to attract attention to the type, but simply to make the text easy to read. One professional summed it up this way:

> "Set running text in one of the hundreds of standard text faces (including humanistic sans serif designs), at a reasonable size — usually between 9- and 12-point. Leave the letter fit alone (don't use tracking), don't enter two spaces between words or sentences, and don't allow justification to enlarge word spaces unreasonably. Use a measure that allows for 60 to 70 characters per line and add a couple of points of leading. Indent paragraphs (all except the first after a heading, anyway) by one em or a pica, and allow for reasonable margins so readers have a place to hold the book. Avoid reader distractions like typewriter quotes and apostrophes or double hyphens where dashes ought to be.
>
> "All these factors work together. If you use a typeface that seems to be harder to read than average—Bodoni, for example—you can compensate by taking pains with spacing, adding leading, or making other adjustments. If you're pretty sure the work will need to be read by people with impaired vision, avoid low contrast and small sizes. If you anticipate poor

> lighting, avoid small type and designs with fine hairlines, and don't use colored inks or papers."

Part of establishing the interior design is the number of words and the number of characters per line. As usual, even published authorities don't always agree on what's best or ideal. There is a consensus that for single column book body text line length should be more than five words and less than fifteen words. The character count is a better criterion, and here is where there is less agreement among experts. Some sources suggest a range of 40 to 75 characters per line. A more typical suggested range is 50 to 75 characters per line, and at least one source cites 65 characters per line as being ideal. This is where you have to balance the choice of typeface (font), type size, and margin widths to achieve an average character count per line that falls within the suggested optimum range. Kathleen Tinkel, quoted above, mentions a study that showed a range of 60 to 70 characters per line made reading easier. That's a good target range, but don't panic if you have a few lines that are 58 characters or a few that are 72 characters.

How do you know what the character count is? You can count each character (and space) in a line manually, but that's work. Word processing software can do the work for you. In TextMaker, it's found under File > Properties > Statistics. The default will display the total number of lines and characters in the entire document. However, if you select a section of text before you choose this function, it will show statistics for the selected text only. To make it easy, select five or ten lines, get the number of characters, and then divide by five or ten to see the number of characters per line.

Especially for print, experimenting with different type faces (fonts) can change the character count per line. In the same type size, different fonts have different character widths and different character spacing. (This is referred to as the "font metrics.")

To save you searching through endless articles and directories of fonts, I have researched numerous articles and sifted the contents to come up with a list of five very readable fonts that seem to make everyone's list for novels and general reading—plus a couple of alternates. The preferred contenders are Baskerville Old Face, Caslon, Georgia, Book Antiqua, and Palatino Linotype.

Another classic typeface that I like very much is Goudy Old Style. Unfortunately, the version of this typeface on my computer does not include true italics. Computer technology can simulate italics by simply slanting the characters, but they don't look nearly as good as an italic font that's designed to harmonize with the corresponding Roman (upright) font. Avoid using any font that doesn't provide true italics.

For text that is likely to be read in poor lighting or by people with poor eyesight, and for textbooks, two other typefaces to consider are Century Schoolbook and Bookman Old Face.

Licenses

We don't tend to think about it, but fonts—or typefaces—are artwork. Each font is different, and each was designed by someone who went through much the same creative process that you went through in writing your book. This means that typefaces are intellectual property and, as such, they can be copyrighted. And most fonts are copyrighted. We are allowed to use fonts in typesetting our books only if we have a license from the owner of the font to use it for the purpose for which we intend to use it.

The most basic collections of fonts that we all have access to consist of whatever fonts came pre-loaded on our computers, usually included with the operating system. Windows includes a large number of fonts, MacOS includes a number of fonts. Linux and iOS include a number of fonts. Many of the fonts included with these operating systems are the same. The publishers of the respective operating systems generally have contracted with the owners of the copyrights to "bundle" the fonts with their operating systems. In turn, the publishers of the operating systems license registered users of the respective operating systems to use the fonts … but only in accordance with the licensing agreement, which—of course—nobody ever reads. This is where it gets sticky.

We think of Microsoft Windows as just "Windows" but, in fact, under Windows 10 there are several different versions:

- Windows 10 Home
- Windows 10 Mobile (for cell phones and small tablets)
- Windows 10 Pro
- Windows 10 Enterprise
- Windows 10 Education
- Windows 10 Mobile Enterprise
- Windows 10 IoT Core

Most of these versions of Windows include the same fonts. However, the End User License Agreement (EULA) is different with respect to the use of the fonts. For versions of Windows intended to home, student, and personal use, the fonts can be used for any personal, non-commercial purpose but they may NOT be used for commercial purposes, nor can they be embedded in PDFs or EPUB files. Selling books is a commercial use; the fonts included with Windows technically can be used for commercial purposes only if your version of Windows is a business version (Windows 10 Pro or Windows 10 Enterprise).

Previous editions of Windows included different assortments of fonts. If you are using an older computer that has gone though updates and upgrades of Windows, it is entirely possible that you may have on your system fonts from an older version of Windows professional even though you are currently using Windows 10 Home.

To make it even more confusing, Microsoft Office also includes fonts, other than those that are included with Windows. And, like Windows, the fonts that come with Microsoft Office are allowed to be used for commercial purposes only if your version of Microsoft Office is a business version: Office 365 Professional, Office Home and Business, or Office Professional. Office 365 Personal and Office Home & Student are not licensed for commercial use.

As I discuss in the next section, not all font licenses are equal. For example, the license from one web site that provides free fonts is completely uninformative: "License: These fonts are neither public domain nor shareware. They may not be transferred to third parties. But we're always pleased when people tell friends and acquaintances about [website] and of course you're welcome to link to us." That tells us precisely nothing whatsoever about the actual terms of the license—so I sent them an e-mail and I asked. The response was the following: "PDF yes, e-book no, webfont no, printing yes, including commercial."

As a result, I had to decide not to use any free fonts from that site, because I can't legally use them to generate e-books. If I can't use a font to create an e-book or a web site—the font is useless.

Don't download it, don't save it, don't even have it on your computer. Find an alternative.

Sources

In the real world, it's extremely unlikely that anyone seeing a book typeset in a font from Microsoft Windows or Microsoft Office will know or care if your version of the software is a home/personal version or a business version. But you should be aware of the distinction, because you may wish to explore fonts other than those already on your computer. There are numerous sites on the Internet from which you can download hundreds of fonts, entirely free. These include, but are not limited to:

- 1001 Fonts
- Font Squirrel
- Fontsov

You have to be careful when downloading fonts from these (and similar) sites, because not all fonts are created equal. These sites don't own the copyrights to the fonts they make available, and the licensing for the fonts isn't the same for all. Some fonts are licensed only for personal use, some are licensed for commercial use in print but not embedded into a e-book, and others may be licensed for all commercial purposes. To keep yourself completely in the clear legally, you should only download fonts that are licensed for all commercial purposes. On Font Squirrel, it appears that all the fonts they list are licensed for all commercial purposes, but it's wise to review the license for each font before downloading it. On Fontsov, you have to check a filter to limit the fonts you see to only those licensed for commercial use. On 1001 Fonts, there's a box toward the upper left on the screen that you have to check to see only fonts licensed for commercial use.

In my case, the computer I am using started out with Windows XP and Microsoft Office Professional 2003. I then upgraded the operating system to Windows 7 and then again to Windows 10, and I have upgraded Microsoft Office to 2010, 2013, 2016, and 2019. Through the upgrades, all the fonts that came with each version have stayed on the computer. The result is that I have a tremendous number of fonts, and I have no idea which of them are licensed for commercial use and which are only for personal use.

When I began self-publishing my writing, I knew that I wanted to feel comfortable that I wasn't infringing on a font designer's copyright by using a font in one of my books that isn't licensed to me for commercial purposes. My solution was to purchase a collection of professional fonts (7,500 of them, in fact) that are all licensed for any and all commercial purposes. This collection was priced at what I considered a very reasonable price (currently $34.95), considering the peace of mind it gives me over the prospect of unwittingly committing font piracy. The collection is named MegaFont NOW and it comes from the German company, SoftMaker (the same company that produces the FreeOffice office suite).

Of course, it isn't necessary to purchase 7,500 fonts to typeset one or even ten books. A tremendous number of those 7,500 fonts are fonts that I will almost certainly never, ever consider using for anything I'm likely to design. For the fonts that I will use, though, I consider it to be money well spent—especially considering that some of the fonts in the collection include outline versions and true small caps.

I'm sure there are other font collections available (in fact, over the years I have previously purchased several). I mention MegaFont NOW as an example of an affordable way to completely avoid questions about the license of the font or fonts you want to use in your book. But that can come later in your career as a writer. For just getting started, you should already have at least a couple or three of the commonly-suggested book fonts already on your computer, so go ahead and use one.

Type Size

An important decision that has to be made is the size of the type used for the body of the book. Kathleen Tinker's article (quoted above) suggests a type size range of 9- to 12-points for body text. Elsewhere in the same article she commented that even 12-point type is large enough that it's on the borderline of becoming difficult to read. On the other hand, the laws of some states stipulate 10-point type as the smallest size allowed for consumer contracts because anything smaller is too difficult for many people to read. I suggest that the range for type size in the body text of most books should be 9.5-point to 11.5-point—and I prefer to stay within the range from 10-point to 11-point.

The selection I quoted (above) from the late Kathleen Tinkel suggests formatting text so that the average line is between 60 and 70 characters (and 65 is often cited as being optimum). Word processing program generally show type sizes in whole numbers in the drop-down menu for selecting type size. That can be overridden. TrueType and OpenType fonts allow them to be increased and decreased in increments of one-half point, so if 10 point is too small but 11 point is too large … just highlight the font size in the style menu and type in "10.5."

What's "right" for your book will be a subjective decision. Some experimentation is needed, because fonts don't all display the same. I recently printed out a sample of two similar fonts; to make them display the same number of characters per line and to appear to be the same size, I had to set one of them in 14-point type and the other in 15-point type.

Select the typeface you want to use, format your body text in that typeface, and then experiment with changing the type size and the line spacing (see below) until the result looks right to you. If possible, print out a couple of sample pages illustrating different combinations and ask friends or relatives which combination looks best to them.

Line Spacing/Leading

Most word processing programs default to setting the type with the lines single-spaced (unless you have changed the settings in the default template). Depending on the typeface selected, standard single-spaced lines may be a little too close together for easiest reading. Articles on typography discuss adding "leading" to increase the vertical distance between lines. However, most word processing software doesn't use the term "leading," but they do allow customizing the space between lines. In TextMaker, this is set in the Format Paragraph dialogue box. Find the setting for Line Spacing, change it from "Single" to "Multiple," and type in a number. "1" is standard single space; I suggest starting with a setting of 1.1 or 1.15—if that's too loose or too tight, adjust up or down in increments of .02 or .05. [Note: In the Line Spacing dialogue box, if you select "At least" or "Exactly," you can then specify the line spacing in points, rather than as a multiple of single spacing.]

An easy test is to save a few pages of your manuscript as a separate file, format that file to the page size, layout, font and font size you are considering, and print two pages. Cut the two pages to the trim size you have chosen, staple them together right at the inside edge of the paper, and then look at it as if you are reading your book. You can do this for multiple options, to experiment with your choices of margins, typeface, font size, and line spacing.

Hyphenation

When text is left-justified, the spaces between words are consistent and each line of text ends where the last full word falls. This is what leads to the ragged, uneven right margins that we call "ragged right." When the style is changed so that body text is fully justified, the word processing software adjusts the spacing between words to bring the last word of each line out to the right-hand margin. Especially in lines that include long words, the result can be that the spaces between the words become too large to look right.

The solution is to use hyphens to break the last word in certain lines so the spaces between the words in the line look more proportionate to the text. All major word processing programs have a way of turning on automatic hyphenation. It should be turned for any documents that will be formatted as fully-justified, and especially for books that will be set fully-justified.

In FreeOffice TextMaker hyphenation is found on the "Layout" tab, in the "Paragraph" panel of the ribbon.

Common Mistakes

The good thing about modern computers, word processing software, and desktop publishing software is that they offer everyone instant access to dozens of professionally-designed fonts. If the fonts that came pre-installed on your computer aren't enough, there are literally thousands of other fonts that can be downloaded for free from the internet.

The bad thing about modern computers, word processing software, and desktop publishing software is that they offer everyone instant access to dozens of professionally-designed fonts. If the fonts that came pre-installed on your computer aren't enough, there are literally thousands of other fonts that can be downloaded for free from the internet.

There is a natural tendency to want to experiment with unusual fonts, and to set different parts of a document in different typefaces. This is usually not a good idea. Years ago I read an article on designing advertising in which the author referred to what he called the "slick but bad presentation." What he was talking about was creating a page, or a single panel on a page, in which the designer used a half dozen or more fonts. The result is something that's too "busy" and jumbled for easy comprehension. Remember, the reason we put words on paper or on a computer screen is to convey information. As the typesetter or page designer, our job is to make the words as easy to read and understand as possible. Throwing too many fonts at the reader just confuses the eye and interferes with reading comprehension.

As I wrote at the start of this chapter, it's best to use only two — or possibly three, at most — fonts throughout a book.

~ ~ ~ ~ ~

Don't use fonts from Google for printed books.

Google Fonts offers fonts that are completely free, BUT … they aren't optimized for print. Google Fonts are optimized for display on a computer screen, tablet, or e-book reader. Can you use them to generate a printed book? Yes, it is possible. However, the quality of the printed results won't be as good as the quality of fonts that were created primarily for printing.

~ ~ ~ ~ ~

Choose typefaces that offer a complete set of fonts.

The two major types of fonts used on computers today are TrueType fonts and OpenType fonts. If you have fonts installed on your computer, they are almost certainly one of these two types. One of the attributes of both TrueType fonts and OpenType fonts is that when the font doesn't offer an actual, designed subset for bold, italic, or bold-italic, the computer can manipulate the font to generate an approximation of any of the above. The quality, however, is not very good. These computer-generated approximations may be tolerable when used in a letter or even an informal report, but they are basically ugly and they

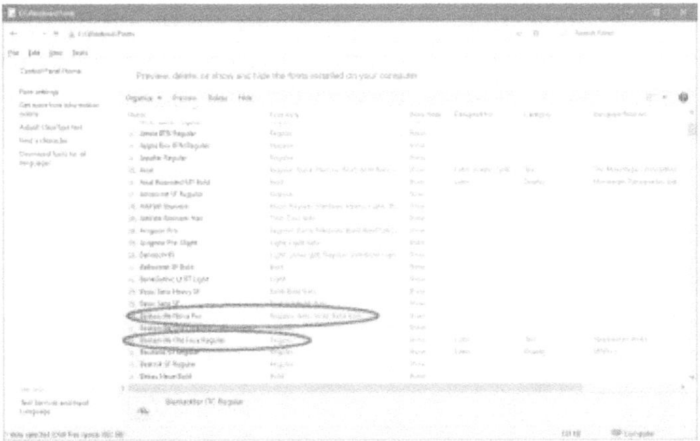

are immediately obvious to any viewer who knows anything at all about either typography or computers.

Try to use only fonts that offer at least four separate files to comprise the font set: a Regular (the standard, upright font that will be used for 90 percent or more of the text), an Italic, a Bold, and a Bold Italic. To see what variations are included with a font, on Windows computers simply open a file explorer application (such as Windows Explorer) and navigate to C:\Windows\Fonts. This will display a list of all the fonts installed on your computer. The second column, "Font Style," shows what variations are included.

Baskerville is a classic typeface that's still a good choice for books. The above image is a screen shot of the font listing on my computer. Notice that the font "Baskerville Old Style" shows that the font family only includes a Regular version. If I were to use this font in a book, anywhere I used italics or boldface type, they would be computer-generated by manipulating the standard "Regular" (Roman, upright) font.

But I have another Baskerville font, Baskerville Nova Pro, which came as part of a collection of "professional" fonts I purchased some time ago. "Baskerville Nova Pro" includes Regular, Italic, Bold, and Bold Italic versions of the font. I have published several books using Baskerville Nova Pro in 11.5-point, with the line spacing set to 1.1.

Here's the difference:

> Lorem ipsum *dolor sit amet*, consectetur adipiscing elit, **sed do** eiusmod tempor incididunt ut ***labore et dolore*** magna aliqua
>
> Lorem ipsum *dolor sit amet*, consectetur adipiscing elit, **sed do** eiusmod tempor incididunt ut ***labore et dolore*** magna aliqua.

The upper passage is set in Baskerville Old Face. Notice how in the italics the vertical strokes are the same shape as in the upright (Roman) font, but manipulated by the computer to be slanted. The bold italic is the same. In the Baskerville Nova Pro type, the italic characters have been specifically designed with rounded serifs and followers to look better as italics.

Computers can also generate "small caps" from standard fonts. These don't look too bad, but a typography professional can usually spot them instantly. Some true "professional" font sets include Small Caps in addition to true Italics, Boldface, and Bolt Italics. Although a professional book designer would never use computer-generated small caps in a commercial book, they get the job done and, in my opinion, they are good enough for at least ninety percent of authors who are self-publishing through the print-on-demand channels. One word of caution about computer-generated small caps, however, is that they may not convert correctly into the EPUB format when exporting the e-book manuscript into the final EPUB version.

I think they are perfectly acceptable for self-published, print-on-demand books, but if you will also publish the same book as an e-book (either Kindle or EPUB), it would be wise to save a separate copy of the manuscript file and eliminate any small caps that were computer-generated.

7 — FINISHING TOUCHES

THERE ARE A COUPLE OF ADDED ENHANCEMENTS that can help to transform your print-on-demand book from something that looks slapped together into something that looks like a "real" book. They aren't difficult to accomplish, and they can help your book stand out from the quick and dirty books churned out by other self-published authors.

Drop Caps

"Drop caps" is short for "dropped capitals," referring to the practice of capitalizing the first letter of a new chapter. In its simplest form, a drop cap uses the same font as the book's body text and simply enlarges it, but there are additional ways to dress up drop caps.

The basic creation of drop caps is built into most word processing programs. In FreeOffice TextMaker, drop caps are found by clicking on the Layout tab and going to the Paragraph panel on the ribbon. In addition to the options for a drop cap of [X] lines in height or setting the drop cap character in the left margin, TextMaker also offers the option of keeping the enlarged character on the same baseline as the rest of the first line and allowing the letter to extend above the first line, rather than below it. TextMaker also allows selecting a different font for the drop cap character.

2

Lorem ipsum dolor sit amet, consectetur adipiscing elit, sed do eiusmod tempor incididunt ut labore et dolore magna aliqua. Posuere lorem ipsum dolor sit amet consectetur adipiscing elit. Eget est lorem ipsum dolor sit amet consectetur. Auctor elit sed vulputate mi sit amet. Leo a diam sollicitudin tempor id. Sodales neque sodales ut etiam sit. Sit amet nisl purus in. Commodo odio aenean sed adipiscing diam donec adipiscing. Non blandit massa enim nec dui nunc mattis. Id nibh tortor id aliquet lectus.

Ipsum suspendisse ultrices gravida dictum fusce ut placerat orci nulla. Facilisis sed odio morbi quis commodo odio. Amet consectetur adipiscing elit

2

Lorem ipsum dolor sit amet, consectetur adipiscing elit, sed do eiusmod tempor incididunt ut labore et dolore magna aliqua. Posuere lorem ipsum dolor sit amet consectetur adipiscing elit. Eget est lorem ipsum dolor sit amet consectetur. Auctor elit sed vulputate mi sit amet. Leo a diam sollicitudin tempor id. Sodales neque sodales ut etiam sit. Sit amet nisl purus in. Commodo odio aenean sed adipiscing diam donec adipiscing. Non blandit massa enim nec dui nunc mattis. Id nibh tortor id aliquet lectus.

Ipsum suspendisse ultrices gravida dictum fusce ut placerat orci nulla. Facilisis sed odio morbi quis commodo odio. Amet consectetur adipiscing elit

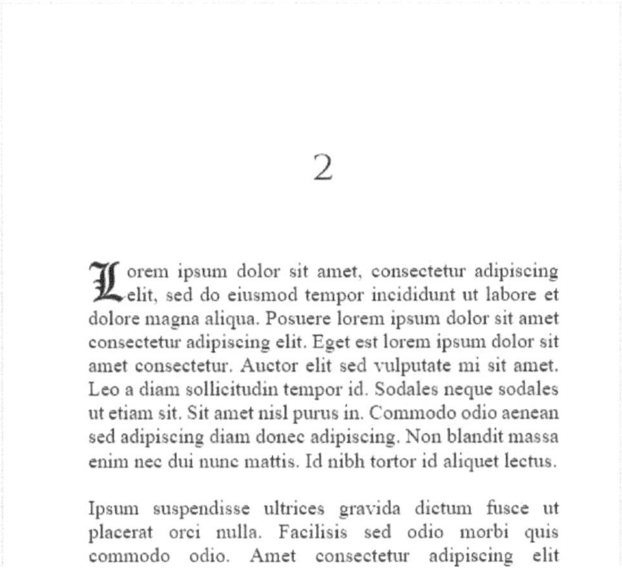

2

Lorem ipsum dolor sit amet, consectetur adipiscing elit, sed do eiusmod tempor incididunt ut labore et dolore magna aliqua. Posuere lorem ipsum dolor sit amet consectetur adipiscing elit. Eget est lorem ipsum dolor sit amet consectetur. Auctor elit sed vulputate mi sit amet. Leo a diam sollicitudin tempor id. Sodales neque sodales ut etiam sit. Sit amet nisl purus in. Commodo odio aenean sed adipiscing diam donec adipiscing. Non blandit massa enim nec dui nunc mattis. Id nibh tortor id aliquet lectus.

Ipsum suspendisse ultrices gravida dictum fusce ut placerat orci nulla. Facilisis sed odio morbi quis commodo odio. Amet consectetur adipiscing elit

All in all, drop caps offer a number of ways to dress up the appearance of your book with nothing more than a few clicks of the mouse.

Small Caps

Just as "Drop Caps" is an abbreviation for "Dropped Capitals," so "Small Caps" is an abbreviation for "Small Capitals." Using small capital letters for the text of the first few words in the first sentence of a new chapter (either alone or in combination with a drop cap) is another way to subtly enhance the typesetting of your book at help convey to the reader that your book wasn't published by a novice.

In professional typesetting, small caps are separate fonts, consisting of all capital characters but approximately two-thirds the height of the standard capital letters in the font. In a true small caps font, the small caps are designed so the stroke widths of the letters are the same as the stroke widths of the full-size characters. Unfortunately, none of the fonts that come standard with Windows or Microsoft Office include true small caps. The good news for self-published authors is that the TrueType and OpenType fonts that come with the operating system can be manipulated to simulate small caps. Professional book designers complain that, because these small caps are scaled down in all respects from their full-size equivalents, the stroke widths aren't the same width. While this is true, the reality is that most readers won't know the difference — especially if your story is good and they are absorbed in the narrative.

2

LOREM IPSUM DOLOR SIT AMET, consectetur adipiscing elit, sed do eiusmod tempor incididunt ut labore et dolore magna aliqua. Posuere lorem ipsum dolor sit amet consectetur adipiscing elit. Eget est lorem ipsum dolor sit amet consectetur. Auctor elit sed vulputate mi sit amet. Leo a diam sollicitudin tempor id. Sodales neque sodales ut etiam sit. Sit amet nisl purus in. Commodo odio aenean sed adipiscing diam donec adipiscing. Non blandit massa enim nec dui nunc mattis. Id nibh tortor id aliquet lectus.

Ipsum suspendisse ultrices gravida dictum fusce ut placerat orci nulla. Facilisis sed odio morbi quis commodo odio. Amet consectetur adipiscing elit

And, of course, small caps can be combined with drop caps:

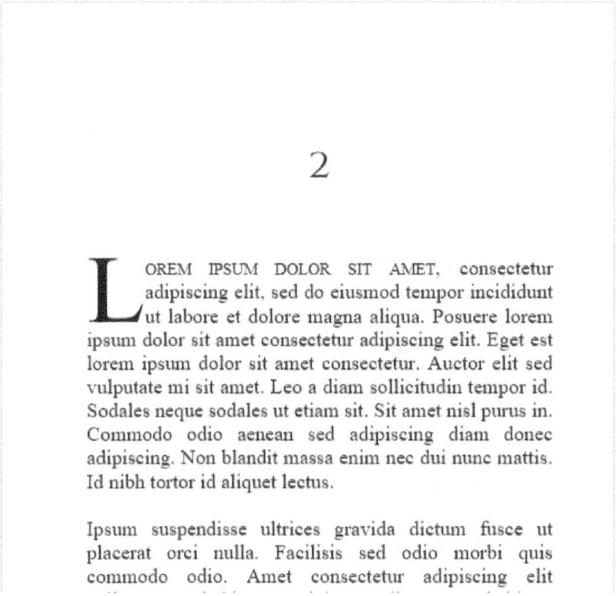

2

LOREM IPSUM DOLOR SIT AMET, consectetur adipiscing elit, sed do eiusmod tempor incididunt ut labore et dolore magna aliqua. Posuere lorem ipsum dolor sit amet consectetur adipiscing elit. Eget est lorem ipsum dolor sit amet consectetur. Auctor elit sed vulputate mi sit amet. Leo a diam sollicitudin tempor id. Sodales neque sodales ut etiam sit. Sit amet nisl purus in. Commodo odio aenean sed adipiscing diam donec adipiscing. Non blandit massa enim nec dui nunc mattis. Id nibh tortor id aliquet lectus.

Ipsum suspendisse ultrices gravida dictum fusce ut placerat orci nulla. Facilisis sed odio morbi quis commodo odio. Amet consectetur adipiscing elit

In FreeOffice TextMaker, select the text you want in small caps. From the Home tab on the ribbon menu, go to the Character panel on the ribbon and click the small arrow at the bottom right corner of the panel. This opens a dialogue box, in which you can click a check box to select Small Caps.

Ligatures

In traditional typesetting, certain combinations of letters tend to run together and type designers back in the days of hand-carved type sometimes designed special blocks that made those combinations a bit fancier. On computers, some TrueType and OpenType fonts include additional glyphs for ligatures. To make your book look just a bit more professional, you may decide to take the time to convert your book to use ligatures if the font you have chosen offers them.

The following illustrates some of the ligatures available in the Times New Roman font:

Aesthetic	Æsthetic
Orthopaedic	Orthopædic
fine	ﬁne
flow	ﬂow
difficult	diﬃcult
affluent	aﬄuent

In this sample, the plain text words are on the left, and the same words with ligatures are in the right-hand column. Using ligatures is completely unnecessary, but those who are willing to expend the time and the effort to use them will have a book that carries another hallmark of having been designed by someone who knows what they're doing.

Unfortunately, putting ligatures into your text is a manual process, and it's tedious. It requires first identifying each ligature you want to use and manually inserting it to a blank line somewhere near the start of the document. This is done from the "Insert" tab on the ribbon, and choosing "Symbol" from the "Text" panel at the right-hand end of the ribbon. The default view will probably be some standard symbols such as the "at" symbol

[@], the glyph for "section" [§], the copyright symbol [©], and a few more. Click on "More" at the bottom to open up the font character map. Be sure the font box at the top shows the font you are using, then scroll through the map to find and select the characters you want. Once you have them available, you can individually copy each one and then use the search and replace function to go through the document and replace each letter combination with the corresponding ligature. Once all the ligatures have been placed, go back and delete the source line that contains just the ligature symbols.

Yes, it's work. Is it worth the time and the effort? For most people and for most books, probably not. For someone who really cares about making their book look as professional as possible, and who can afford to take the time to do it — it's a nice, subtle touch to set your work apart for everyone else.

~ ~ ~ ~ ~

As with most enhancements, if you overdo them they just look busy or fussy. Don't overdo. Used with restraint, drop caps and small caps can make a huge difference in making your book look like a professional product rather than the slap-dash effort of an amateur.

8 — FRONT MATTER

AS AUTHORS, we expend copious amounts of time and effort on creating, editing, and perfecting the text that comprises the body of our books. When a book is published, however, before the reader ever gets to the book itself there is a bunch of miscellaneous information that comes before the actual text of the book. Since this assemblage of miscellany is located at the front of the book, it is cleverly referred to as the "front matter." There are lists of what items go into the front matter and, naturally, not all authorities agree on the order in which they are presented. Also, depending on the type of book and the author's wishes and intentions, some front matter items are optional and may not be used at all.

What goes into the front matter?

- The title page (mandatory)
- The copyright page (mandatory)
- The dedication page (optional, but customary)
- Table of Contents (usually only in non-fiction books)
- An epigraph (optional)
- A preface (optional but customary)
- A foreword (optional)

Especially for print books, to the above list may be added

- A half title page (optional)
- A frontispiece (optional)

- An acknowledgements page
- A list of tables (non-fiction, optional)
- A list of illustrations (non-fiction, optional)
- An introduction
- Another half title page

What are these, and how should they be arranged? The following pages will explain what they are. The order in which I will discuss them is the order suggested by one of the sources I reviewed for what order the front matter should follow. As I commented above, not all sources agree on either the order of the items to be included. To facilitate my research, I entered into a spreadsheet the various items in the suggested order as cited in seven different web sites discussing publishing. One list, from TheBookDesigner.com, is more extensive than any of the others, so I am going to follow the order in which that site organized and discussed them.

Note that in print, the pages comprising the front matter are numbered using lower case Roman numerals rather than Arabic numbers. Pages such as the title page and copyright page are not numbered; the first numbered page should be the first page after the copyright page, whether that's a dedication page,

Half Title Page

The title and the author's name both appear, of course, on the cover (or on the jacket, in the case of many hardcover books). In mass market paperbacks and many low-end and self-published paperback books, the first printed page is often the title page. In higher quality books, however, to sort of set the stage for the interior title page the book designer may make the first right-hand page a half title page. (Or the first right-hand page may simply be left blank.)

A half title page simply repeats the book's title, but not the author's name or any other information), usually using the same font or fonts as the title page but reduced in size/scale to two-thirds or one-half size. Its purpose is to provide a transition into the book.

I would not use a half title page for an e-book version.

The Frontispiece

A frontispiece is a page containing an illustration that sets the tone for a book and is almost always placed (if used) on the first left-hand page, facing the title page. This means that if your book layout doesn't include either a first half title page or a blank first page, there will not be a left-hand page facing the title page and you can't use a frontispiece illustration.

The use of a frontispiece is always optional. There is especially no reason for it in an e-book.

The Title Page

While a half title page is optional, the actual title page is not optional. The title page includes the full title of the book, the author's name, and may also include the name (and possibly the logo) of the publisher. The layout and type style of the title page usually mirrors that of the outer cover, but title pages usually don't include the artwork (if the cover includes artwork). Unlike a half title page, on the title page the book title is not reduced in size or scale; both the title and the author's name should appear at approximately the same size and layout as on the outer cover.

The Copyright Page

Especially if you have copyrighted your book, the copyright page is not optional. This is the page on which the author (or other copyright owner, if applicable) states the copyright and the year in which the copyright was created. The copyright page is always the left-hand page immediately following the title page.

The copyright page is also where the publication information is placed. This includes the Library of Congress Control Number (LCCN), if you obtained one, the ISBN number, any legal disclaimers (such as, for example, something like, "This is a work of fiction. Any resemblance between the characters in this book and real persons, living or dead, is accidental and coincidental.") The copyright page should also include the publisher's full name, physical address, and (if applicable) mailing address. You may want to also include a web site address.

It is important to understand that any disclaimer you place on the copyright page is a legal statement. You put it there for the purpose of avoiding legal liability, such as for inadvertently libeling someone. If you can possibly afford it, it would be wise to have an attorney either draft or, at least, review the language of your disclaimer. If you can't afford to use an attorney, take the time to review and copy the disclaimers of as many books in your genre as possible. Write down the exact language, or take photos for reference. Look at the disclaimers in books from larger publishing houses rather than from indie self-publishers. The big publishing houses will have had their disclaimers drafted by corporate lawyers, so those will be the best examples on which to base your disclaimer.

The Dedication

Not every book has a dedication. If you choose to dedicate your book to someone, all that's needed is a simple paragraph, or even just one sentence. The dedication goes on the right-hand page facing the copyright page; a dedication usually comes before an epigraph, or a table of contents.

The Epigraph

An epigraph, if used, is a quotation that sets the tone for the book. An epigraph is optional. Some authors may choose to omit an epigraph in the front matter and, instead, place a brief epigraph at the beginning of each chapter. The choice is yours.

If I use an epigraph, I prefer to put it on the next right-hand page following the dedication. Many book designers, though, place the epigraph on the left-hand page facing either the table of contents, or the first page of the book body.

The Table of Contents

A table of contents is optional, for both print and digital formats. That said, my view is that it's never a bad idea to include a hyperlink table of contents for fiction, to allow readers to jump immediately to a specific chapter. For fiction in print, I don't think a table of contents is at all necessary. Where a table of contents is called for is in non-fiction and technical books, in which a reader might want to be able to open directly to a specific topic.

All the major word processing programs include the ability to automatically generate a table of contents, based on they styles used for the chapter headings and subheads. This is another very good reason to learn to use text styles to define your text rather than always leaving the style set to "Normal" or "Default" and then applying the style characteristics manually. Depending on the structure of your book, a table of contents may list only chapters, or it may be broken down into chapters and then sections within chapters.

The List of Figures

In publishing, "figures" refers to illustrations. These may be photographs, drawings, sketches, maps—any sort of graphic image. They may or may not include captions. If a book includes a large number of illustrations, it can be helpful to include a list of figures following the table of contents. If you do so, the list should include the figure number, a descriptive title (if the caption is too long), and for print books it should include the page number.

The List of Tables

Most books won't include many tables, so this won't be necessary. If your book does happen to include a large number of tables, it may be helpful to readers to include a list of tables that's separate from the table of contents and the list if figures. If you include a list of tables, it should be set up the same as the list of figures.

The Foreword

A foreword is a short essay written about the book by someone other than the author. A foreword is optional, and is perhaps more commonly used for non-fiction books rather than for fiction. If used, a foreword should be brief—typically one page, and not more than two pages. If used, a foreword should end with the name of the person who wrote it, the date, and the place of residence of the person who wrote the foreword.

As a rule, a foreword should be written by a recognized authority in the field covered by the book, and it should explain why the contents of the book will be of value to the reader in expanding their understanding of the topic or the field. Because the time of recognized experts in any technical field is valuable, unless you are an expert who has other experts as close, personal friends, it is customary for writers of forewords to be paid. The amount of the payment is a function of the fame and reputation of the author of the foreword, your own reputation in the field, the length of the foreword, and the value the foreword is likely to add to the book. A typical range might be between $100 and $500; do not blithely reach out to the world's foremost expert in your topic and expect that he or she will be overjoyed to write a foreword for you—an unknown in the field—out of the goodness of their heart.

The Preface

A preface is similar to a foreword, except that a preface is written by the author of the book. Like the foreword, a preface is optional. A preface is typically found in non-fiction books rather than in novels.

Authors may use a preface to explain how the book came into being: where they got the idea to write it, the reasons for writing it, the author's qualifications in the subject matter of the book, and perhaps a brief discussion of any research methodologies employed in compiling the material that comprises the book.

Also like a foreword, a preface should be brief—one or two pages, at most.

If you include a preface, use it to tell readers why they should read your book. Use the preface to share your excitement about the subject matter, and let them know what they'll gain by reading your book.

Acknowledgements

Most authors consult with someone during the course of writing a book, either for research into matters the author doesn't fully understand, or editors and "beta" readers who helped review and polish the manuscript into its final form. The acknowledgements section is where the author lets readers know who helped him/her, and how, and where the author expresses thanks to those people.

The Introduction

An introduction is usually used in non-fiction books. The introduction can be used to inform the reader about how the book is organized, and what are the purposes and goals of the book. In teaching, instructors are advised to begin a class by explaining to the students what they are going to learn, then go on to teach the material, and then to end the class by reminding the students what they have just learned. The introduction to a book serves the same purpose as the first of the three parts of teaching: use the introduction to "tee up" the material, to prepare your readers for the more detailed information that will follow in the individual chapters.

How is the introduction different from the preface? The preface should be about you, the author, and the process of creating the book. The introduction is about the subject matter of the book. It's essentially a chapter before the first chapter, which is why it is part of the front matter rather than part of the book body.

The Prologue

Whereas an introduction is usually found in non-fiction books, fiction books often include a prologue to set the stage for the events that will take place in the body of the book. A prologue is the author's opportunity to relate the back story that's not part of the events in the book but which led up to the point in time where and when the book begins. In some cases, the prologue may also be a place to introduce one or two of the main characters—or it may be set far enough in the past that it introduces instead the ancestors of the book's main characters.

Authorities don't agree on whether a prologue belongs with the front matter, or with the book body. The only functional difference is whether a prologue (if you use one) is placed before or after the second half title page, and whether it gets numbered using lower case Roman numerals or Arabic numbers.

The Second Half Title Page

If you used a half title page just inside the front cover, then you might also want to use a second half title page to separate the front matter from the body of the book. If used, the second half title page should be an exact duplicate of the first half title page. The second half title page should not have a header, footer, or page number; it should only include the title of the book.

9 — PREPARING FOR PUBLICATION

WHEN SUBMITTING THE FINISHED MANUSCRIPT to an on-line publishing service, it is important to submit the file in a format the publisher will accept. The file requirements for printed books are generally different from the requirements for e-books, and not all e-books use the same format. Before uploading your manuscript, be sure that your manuscript file is in the correct format, and that you have checked it for errors.

Amazon KDP can accept manuscript files in the following formats for the interior of printed books: PDF, RTF, DOCX, TXT, EPUB, and HTML. Cover files for printed books must be in PDF format, or you can use KDP's on-line Cover Creator to generate your cover

Barnes and Noble Press has time constraints on uploads. Manuscript and cover files for printed books must be uploaded at least ten days before the scheduled date of publication. For the interior of printed books, Barnes and Noble Press will accept files in the DOCX, TXT, RTF, HTML and PDF formats. Cover files for printed books must be in PDF format; JPG and other graphics file formats are not accepted.

Draft2Digital (D2D) accepts the following files types for book interiors: .DOC, .DOCX, .RTF, .OTF, and TXT for either print or e-book. D2D also accepts files in the .PDF format for printed books. According to the D2D web site, the .DOCX format is the most popular.

Table of Contents

For printed books, a table of contents is not usually needed or provided for novels. Tables of contents (as well as indexes) are more commonly found in non-fiction, technical and reference books. For a non-fiction technical or reference book that calls for a table of contents in the print version, the table of contents will not be hyperlinked but will include page number references for each chapter and section listed in the table of contents. The major word processing programs all include a function for generating a table of contents based on the use of paragraph styles to define chapter and section headings. I very much recommend using this automated table of contents generation function rather than trying to laboriously go through a long manuscript to find each chapter and subhead, copy the title to the table of contents, and then manually enter the page number.

To avoid having to repeat the process after making editorial changes, I suggest saving the table of contents step for the end. Don't generate the table of contents until the manuscript has been completed and edited, and (for printed books) after the book interior has been completely formatted to the desired trim size, typeface, and font size. Otherwise, the page numbers will be incorrect.

In TextMaker a table of contents is easy to create:

1. Position the text cursor at the beginning of the line in which the table of contents should be placed.
2. Choose the ribbon command "References" | group "Table of contents" | "Generate."

As soon as you confirm with "OK," the table of contents is inserted into the text. If a table of contents already exists, it will be updated at the existing position. For example:

Excerpt from a table of contents

TextMaker displays the headings on the left. To the right of each heading, the corresponding page number is displayed.

Converting the File for Upload

For printed books, although most of the print-on-demand services accept files in the Microsoft Word .DOCX format, they also all accept files in the .PDF format. I prefer to upload PDFs, because that gives me an opportunity to see what the final book is going to look like before I even upload the file and submit it to the service's quality check. FreeOffice TextMaker includes a function to export to PDF.

When converting the book interior to PDF for upload, especially if you have used fonts that were not included with your computer's operating system, be sure to learn how to embed the fonts in the PDF file. This is important because, even with a PDF file, if the fonts in the document aren't installed on the computer on which the file is being read, the system will substitute another font that it (the computer) thinks is the best near-equivalent. The substitute font is almost never going to be a true equivalent, so substitute fonts will wreak havoc on the formatting of your book.

Amazon KDP requires that fonts be embedded in the file you upload for print.

In FreeOffice TextMaker, the Export to PDF menu choice opens a dialogue box with multiple tabs. The "Preferences" tab offers an option to embed fonts, and a separate option for PDF/A (which is disabled and not available in the FreeOffice version of TextMaker]. Choosing to embed fonts but not selecting PDF/A will embed fonts but not include other features of the PDF/A archival standard. For the purpose of uploading a file for print-on-demand publishing, the other features of the PDF/A standard are not important. Just be sure to choose to embed fonts.

10 — A WORD ABOUT ISBNs

ISBN IS THE ACRONYM for International Standard Book Number. An ISBN is to books much like a VIN (Vehicle Identification Number) is to an automobile. It isn't a legal requirement for a book to have an ISBN, but in practical terms a book can't be sold without one, because the ISBN is how booksellers find, order, and stock books and it is also how most libraries catalog books. Unless you are writing a book for the sole purpose of having a few copies printed to give away to family and friends … you need an ISBN.

Each unique version of a book needs its own ISBN. This means that if you publish the same book in hardcover, trade (quality) paperback, and "mass market" paperback formats, you will need three ISBNs. E-books (Amazon Kindle, Barnes & Noble Nook, Kobo, Apple Books and others) do not require an ISBN. However, although other sources disagree, the director of my local public library as told me that most libraries acquire and catalog e-books by ISBN, so his recommendation is to assign a unique ISBN to digital editions, as well. Since a unique ISBN is required for each unique format of a title, this would mean one ISBN for a Kindle edition and a separate ISBN for an EPUB edition.

ISBNs are not distributed by the government, at least in the United States. In the United States, ISBN numbers are purchased through the ISBN provider R. R. Bowker, LLC. In the U.S.,

ISBNs have a cost, and it's not cheap. In fact, for self-publishing on a budget, purchasing the ISBN may be the single most expensive item in the process. Bowker charges $125 for a single ISBN. The unit price drops considerably if you purchase multiple ISBNs; Bowker currently offers ten ISBNs for $295, and blocks of 100 ISBNs for $575. Bowker also maintains the catalog of books in print, so an advantage to buying your own ISBNs from Bowker is that you can ensure that your book is listed in the industry-standard catalog as being in print and available — and that you are listed as the publisher.

In the United Kingdom and the Republic of Ireland, Nielsen Book Services Ltd is the ISBN distributor. Just to be different, Canada has one source for books in English and a separate provider in Quebec for books in French: Library and Archives Canada, and Bibiolthèque et Archives Nationales du Québec. Both can be accessed through a common Internet portal. In the U.K. and Ireland, Nielsen operates much like Bowker in the U.S.; a single ISBN costs £89.00, a block of ten costs £164.00, and a block of 100 costs £369.00. ISBNs for self-publishers who are permanent residents of Canada are free.

Whether or not to buy a single ISBN or a block of ISBNs depends on personal preferences. Both Amazon and Barnes & Noble ask authors if they have an ISBN for their book at the time the book is uploaded. If not, Amazon and Barnes & Noble will provide an ISBN — at no cost to the author. One problem with this is that the entity that owns the ISBN is officially the publisher so if you allow Amazon KDP to provide the ISBN for your print-on-demand book, Amazon KDP will forever be listed as the publisher. You will still own the copyright and you will still be listed as the author, but you will NOT be the publisher.

A second problem is confusion. If you publish the exact same book through Amazon KDP and through Barnes & Noble Press, each will assign an ISBN to the book in their system. Now you will have two ISBNs and two publishers associated with the same book. In my opinion, while accepting a free ISBN is obviously the cheapest way to get published (unless you are in Canada), it makes sense only if you never plan to offer the book through more than one service — or if you don't care about sales, and you just want to be able to have some books printed to give away.

The question of whether or not to assign ISBNs to digital books is even murkier. Despite what my library director told me, the vast majority of e-book authors do not assign ISBNs to their e-books. Their view is that most of their sales and circulation will be directly through Amazon and Amazon doesn't require an ISBN, so why spend money on something that's unnecessary? That logic is difficult to refute.

In the end, it's a personal choice.

11 — COVERS

A BOOK ISN'T COMPLETE WITHOUT A COVER. You can be the best writer in the universe, and it won't matter if people don't pick up your book and start reading it. So how do you entice people to buy your book?

The answer is: with a great cover. Of course, we have probably all also heard the saying, "You can't judge a book by its cover." But, in reality, isn't that exactly what we do as readers? There are a lot of books in the world. Even if you know what genre you're looking for—such as Romance—if you walk into a bookstore and go to the Romance aisle, or you log onto Amazon and search for "Books - Romance," you will still be confronted by an assortment of literally hundreds of books. You only want to buy one—how do you decide which one?

If you are like me, you probably start by simply scanning the covers, looking at the covers and the titles for the ones that strike a chord with you on some visceral level. Once you have identified a few covers that might be worthy of your consideration, then you probably turn over the book to read the blurb on the back cover (in a physical bookstore) or click on the title to read the blurb on-line.

A basic rule for cover design, perhaps especially in fiction, is that you don't want your cover to be too different from other books of the same genre. Obviously, you don't want your cover to look exactly like another book, but you don't want to style or design of your cover to be so radically different from the others in the same genre that your cover looks amateurish or is clearly the odd man out in the bunch.

Book cover design is a specialty so, unless you have some graphic arts capabilities, this is one aspect of self-publishing where it may be better to pay a professional rather than going it alone—if you can afford to hire a professional. Not everyone can afford that, and since this book is about getting your book self-published using nothing but free software, let's discuss ways to create your cover for free.

Many of the low-budget cover artists don't create original art for the covers they design; they download a photo or two or three from the Internet, use a program such as Adobe *PhotoShop* to combine and manipulate the images, and then they paste the title over the cover image. Despite what the "experts" say, a budget publisher who has some sense of aesthetics and composition can create a perfectly acceptable book cover using the free Microsoft Paint or Paint 3-D program that comes with Windows. Most versions ("distros") of the Linux operating system include the GIMP graphics program, which has a steep learning curve but is ultimately much more capable than Windows Paint. And there are other Paint-like programs that can be downloaded for free.

Using Paint has a significant handicap: The text. In Windows Paint, you can create a text box, type in or paste in text, and as long as you keep that text box active you can move it around, change the font, the font size, the font color ... but as soon as you click the mouse anywhere *outside* of the text box, that text becomes an integral part of the image and it can't be re-opened for editing.

That's a problem. One solution is to use the cover creator provided by Amazon KDP when you upload the book body. It works, but the cover generally comes out looking like it was designed by Amazon KDP. I have never been happy with Amazon-generated covers but it's free, so it's definitely worth a look. If you can come up with a cover you're happy with, you don't need to look any farther. But what if you're not happy with Amazon's cover creator?

Instead, how about using the same TextMaker program you used to write and format the book interior to also do the book cover? The purists will tell you it's just not possible to make an acceptable cover using just a word processor, but the reality is that it's easier with *PhotoShop,* but it's entirely possible using just TextMaker. The print-on-demand services prefer a PDF file, and TextMaker can export to PDF, so it's certainly possible from a technical perspective. The free version of TextMaker has one disadvantage when trying to make a cover for a printed book, which I'll discuss when we get there, but it can be overcome by using Microsoft Paint or any similar program.

Where do we start? As the King told Alice in Wonderland, "It is best to begin at the beginning."

The first step, as with formatting the book size, is to set TextMaker for the page size. But a printed book has a front cover, a back cover, and a spine. Before you can lay out a cover, you have to know the thickness of the spine. That's a function of the number of pages and the paper type, so the interior layout has to be completed and finalized before starting the cover layout. Once you know the number of pages, Amazon KDP offers an on-line cover calculator that will automatically generate a template with all the dimensions you need to know in designing your book cover.

As an example, assume the trim size is 5.5" x 8.5". For covers, we usually want to ensure that the image or background color extend all the way to the edges, so KDP requires 1/8-inch of extra space (called "bleed") around the perimeter. This means the height for the cover will be 8.5+.125+.125 = 8.75 inches.

The width has to include the front cover, the back cover, the spine, and the bleed on each edge. If the book thickness comes out as one-half inch, the total width for the cover will be .125+5.5+.5+5.5+.125 = 11.75 inches. As you did for the book interior, open up TextMaker to a new blank document, go into the page layout dialogue box, and set the required dimensions from the Amazon template (including the bleed) as a custom page size. The page will be wider than it is high, so be aware that if you set the larger number as the width, the orientation should still be Portrait. If you set the smaller dimension as the width, the orientation should then be set to Landscape.

Go to the margins settings and set the page margins to zero on all sides. THIS IS IMPORTANT!

With the page set up, the next step is to import the photo or image you want to use as the background for the cover. You can have any number of image boxes, so it is possible to use one image for the front and a different image for the back. For simplicity, I prefer to find a single photo or image in landscape (horizontal) orientation that has the important part of the image on the right-hand side, and make that my cover image.

On the "Insert" tab, look in the "Objects" panel for "Picture." When you click on that, from the pop-up menu choose "From file ..." This opens a file manager that allows you to search for the image on your computer or cloud service. When you find the image you want, click "Open" at the lower right corner on the window. The image will be pasted into the page. With the margins set to zero, the image should completely fill either the width or the height of the cover area. Unless you are very lucky and the proportions of the photo happen to match the proportions of your cover exactly, the image probably won't extend to the edges completely in both height and width.

The image will have small circles at all four corners and on the mid-points of the sides. These are called "handles." If you allow the mouse cursor to hover over one of these circles, you should see it turn into an arrow. Clicking and dragging these handles allows you to resize the image. However, the default setting is for resizing the preserve the proportions of the image. This is called locking the "aspect ratio." If you use the mouse to drag one side smaller, you'll see that the height also becomes smaller.

To get the image to completely fill the cover, you need to unlock the aspect ratio. To do this, right click somewhere inside the image. At the bottom of the pop-up menu, click on "Picture properties ..." From the Picture Properties dialogue box, you can adjust virtually everything about the image. To unlock the aspect ratio, go to the "Format" tab and uncheck the box for "Keep aspect ratio." Click "OK" to close the dialogue box, and you can now resize the height and width of the image independently. Drag the handles to the edge of the cover on all four sides.

The most difficult part of getting a cover right is defining the spine area and keeping the text within that. TextMaker makes that easier by providing a way to draw guidelines that you can use to define the spine. From the "Insert" tab, click "Lines" in the "Objects" panel, then click on the selection for a plain, straight line.

The back cover will be 5.5" + .125" (the bleed, remember?), so the left edge of the spine will be at 5.625" from the left edge. The top ruler starts at zero, so the first line will be drawn from the top of the page under the 5.625 tic on the ruler, straight down the page. On the bottom edge of the screen there is a box that shows the position of the cursor relative to the left edge and top edge of the page. This makes it easy to start the line and keep it vertical as you drag the mouse to the bottom of the page.

The spine is half an inch wide, so we need a second line at 5.625" + .5" = 6.125. Draw a second vertical line at 6.13 inches. This establishes where the spine will be. Don't worry about the lines ruining the cover — they'll be erased at the end. Remember that there's an eighth of an inch of "bleed" at the edges, and if the book is bound and trimmed perfectly that goes away during manufacture. The actual margin allowance begins an eighth of an inch from the edges. If you need the extra visual guidance, you can also draw in those guidelines.

Once the guidelines have been placed, it's time to enter the text. I typically begin with the title. Once again, go to the "Insert" tab and the "Objects" panel. Right next to the "Picture" icon is the icon for "Text frame." Click that. Place the mouse cursor approximately where you want the upper left corner of the text frame to be, click and hold the left mouse button, and drag the cursor down and to the right to create the frame. It will have handles, so once it's in place you can adjust the size, and move it around.

Inserting the text frame opens up the standard word processing tools, allowing you to select the justification (usually center), the font, the type size, and the type color. Type in your title, and make any changes needed to make it what you want. You will be able to return to it and make changes later, if necessary. Repeat this to create a new text box for the author's name, and another text box on the back cover for the blurb and/or a paragraph about the author.

With the title, author, and blurb entered, it's time to add the title and the author to the spine. Note that very thin books won't provide enough space on the spine, so it may have to be left blank. The KDP cover template tells you the actual width of the cover and it also gives the dimension for the spine "safe" zone. This is because the cover may shift slightly during the binding of the book, and they don't want the spine text so close to the edge that the slight shift will result in the text bending around onto the front or back cover. Be sure to keep the safe zone in mind.

In order to put text on the spine, we need to make another text box, enter the title again, rotate it 90 degrees, and move it to the spine. Fortunately, TextMaker makes that easy.

Create a new test frame, the same as above. Type in the title, using the same font as on the front cover, and adjust the font *size* to approximately what you think will fit within the spine safe zone. Click anywhere outside of the text box to get out of edit mode, click inside the text box again to make the outline and handles active, then move the mouse cursor over the text box until you see the cursor change to the crossed arrow symbol for dragging the text box. Instead of dragging it, right click once to open a pop-up menu, and click on "Properties" at the bottom of the menu.

In the "Properties" dialogue window, click on the 'Inner text" tab toward the right-hand side. At the lower left, there is a panel that allows you to choose the text orientation. Click on the orientation you want, then click "Okay." The text box will now be rotated to the correct orientation. You can drag it into position, resize the text as needed, and fine-tune the position until the text falls neatly into the spine safe zone.

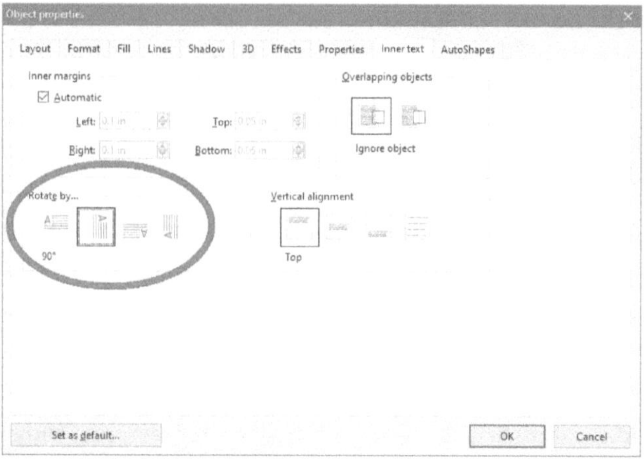

Repeat this process to put the author's name on the spine.

The cover is now finished. All that's left to do is to save it, then export it to PDF using the built-in export function, the same as for the book body.

The following image is a sample book cover I created using the exact procedure spelled out in this chapter:

12 — CONCLUSION

FORMATTING A BOOK FOR PRINT isn't rocket science. The difference between a book that looks grossly amateurish and a book that looks like it was designed by someone who knows what they're doing is generally just a matter of paying attention to details that are easily addressed using most major word processing programs.

There are a lot of books for sale on Amazon's web site, so new authors are competing against a huge field. You should expect that prospective buyers will use Amazon's "Look Inside" feature to see what's behind the cover of your book. They can't read the whole story, but they can usually read the first chapter, or at least a good portion of it. The story itself has to be good enough to grab and hold their interest, but how they view the story may also be affected by their subconscious reaction to the appearance of the book itself. If it looks sloppy and unprofessional, that perception is going to color their perception of the story — whether they recognize it or not.

Many years ago, in the auto racing field, Roger Penske became famous for finding new ways to give his teams an advantage. His little ways to gain an edge were always within the rules, they were just things that the other teams hadn't thought of. In any competitive endeavor, you can't afford to give your competitors an advantage. Having a professional-looking book is certainly an advantage. If your competitors are doing it, you can't afford not to do the same. You owe it to yourself, and you owe it to your story.

It is my hope that this little book will help new writers to realize that it isn't difficult to produce professional-looking books, so they can compete on even terms with other authors in their chosen genre. Most important, creating professional-looking books doesn't require spending money to buy new software, or using valuable writing time to learn a new software program. Even if you are on an extremely tight budget, by using *free* software such as FreeOffice and the information contained in this book, anyone can self-publish a professional-looking book to Amazon KDP or to any of the competing print-on-demand services with *zero* out-of-pocket expense (other than possibly purchasing an ISBN number).

ABOUT THE AUTHOR

Harwood W. Loomis is a semi-retired architect, ordained minister, clinical hypnotherapist, and author whose technical articles have appeared in a number of trade magazines dedicated to architecture, engineering, and property management. A lifelong automotive hobbyist, he has crewed for a stock car racing team, built his own race car for competition on the New England hillclimb circuit, and he is a former state champion in the Connecticut Council of Sports Car Clubs autocross series.

Harwood is a Vietnam veteran. His awards from his service in the United States Army include the Army Commendation Medal, Army Good Conduct Medal, Vietnam Service Medal with Two Bronze service Stars, Meritorious Unit Commendation, Republic of Vietnam Gallantry Cross Unit Citation with Palm Device, and the Republic of Vietnam Civil Actions Honor Medal Unit Citation, First Class. During his Army career he was a member of the 1814 Color Guard and a member of his battalion competition shooting team.

Harwood has served as a member of the board of directors and Vice President of Cornerstone, a mental health halfway house in New Haven, Connecticut; member of the board of directors, author, and contributing editor for the Trumbull [Connecticut] PC Users Group; and member of the board of directors and newsletter editor for The Phenix Society, a not-for-profit organization dedicated to improving the quality of life for senior citizens. He currently acts as a moderator on three Internet discussion forums and writes for and serves as Senior Editor for an on-line magazine.

Harwood is a widower who lives with his family of Jeep Cherokees and Jeep Comanches in Woodbridge, Connecticut. His house stands on the last remaining portion of a larger tract of land that was granted to a maternal ancestor by King George of England before the American Revolution. He qualifies for membership in the Sons of the American Revolution as a result of service during the revolution by both maternal and paternal ancestors.

TO LEARN MORE ABOUT SELF-PUBLISHING

There is a lot more to successful self-publishing than just the layout of the book's interior. If you found the information in this book to be helpful, you might enjoy my larger book, *The Frugal Yankee's Guide To Self-Publishing*. That book is available in both paperback and e-book versions, from Amazon and multiple other outlets.

https://www.amazon.com/Frugal-Yankees-Guide-Self-Publishing-ebook/dp/B09QLBG9X3/ref=sr_1_9?crid=3TUWK02EZZ2TS&keywords=books+by+Harwood+Loomis&qid=1686999642&s=books&sprefix=books+by+harwood+loomis%2Cstripbooks%2C106&sr=1-9

Made in United States
Cleveland, OH
04 November 2026

47642852R00058